Beyond the Guano: A Yelapa Memoir

DW Risdon

Beyond the Guano: A Yelapa Memoir

Copyright © 2016 DW Risdon

All rights reserved.

ISBN-13: 978-0692623244
ISBN-10: 0692623248

DEDICATION

TO MY WIFE, DIANNE, WHOSE NOMADIC SPIRIT MAKES EVERY DAY AN ADVENTURE.

Beyond the Guano: A Yelapa Memoir

CONTENTS

	Acknowledgments	i
	Prologue	1
1	The Second Year	5
2	The Third Year	91
3	The Fourth Year	170
4	Retiring in Yelapa	182
	Epilogue	200

Beyond the Guano: A Yelapa Memoir

ACKNOWLEDGMENTS

A special thank you, (gracias) to the warm and giving people of Yelapa, without whom these stories could not have been written.

Beyond the Guano: A Yelapa Memoir

Prologue

One Sunday afternoon, I am summoned to our living room. My wife, Dianne, browses an issue of Sunset magazine on loan from the local library. The open page features a remote village on the southern edge of Banderas Bay. Its name is Yelapa.

I chuckle, then comment that I visited Yelapa thirty years ago. My recollection is one of a charming, somewhat primitive, jungle village with pristine beaches and cold beer. Thirty days later, Dianne and I exit the airport in Puerto Vallarta, hail a cab and board a water taxi heading to Yelapa. Our lodging host greets us at the town pier and within thirty minutes, we trek along the main path towards an evening of fun, food and frolic.

We return the following May. Guided by our local host, we visit rental properties and lease a two-bedroom apartment with patio. Dianne and I head back home, liquidate household belongings, sell two vehicles and market the house. Just shy of a year from our first visit, we stand at LAX with six plastic totes, a dog crate, a guitar case, a computer case and two backpacks.

Let the adventure begin!

The events that follow are the bounty from which blogs are born. Our first year is spent adjusting and settling. The blog, Yelapa Memo, begins after our return the second season. Be forewarned, all anecdotes bear a sprinkling of creativity; yet always include some thread of truth. We experience warm and friendly people, incredible food and drink, and a physical environment right out of the Nature Channel.

To assist those, like us, who consider resettling internationally for a portion of their golden years, I offer a dedicated section "Retiring in Yelapa." The information is generic and applies to re-settling anywhere in the world.

Welcome to Yelapa. *Bienvenido a Yelapa.*

About the cover: All who visit Yelapa pass a massive monolith on the eastern edge of our bay. It temporarily blocks any view of the village. Locals refer to this landmark as "shit rock." On any given day, passersby spy pelicans, egrets, herons, boobies, or frigate birds. All engage in refreshing the rock's white-washed appearance. This memoir addresses our life *Beyond the Guano.*

Chapter 1
The Second Year

Viva (October)

Soon, the Yelapa Memo Blog will spring to life and share everyday happenings in our village. Be forewarned, stories contain substantial amounts of tongue-in-cheek. If you want specifics regarding lodging, dining, water taxi schedules or weather, there are sites available. I suggest you visit TripAdvisor.com. Scan the comments of others.

October finds the population of twelve hundred abuzz. Everyone paints, plasters, buffs and shines everything. This includes, on occasion, slow moving dogs. Restaurant owners scour kitchens and patios in preparation for opening night. Water taxi receive fresh paint and expand their schedules for increased traffic. We are busy people. Did you think that paradise just happened?

If you are a reasonable human being when you journey to Yelapa, please stay that way. Dress is casual. A pair of shorts, t-shirt, and flip-flops will work. All three are necessary, two out of three will generate disdain. Enjoy your favorite beverage either in the numerous restaurants or in your *casita*. Our cobblestone paths and hills are not friendly to those who abandon control of their balance. Enough said.

Kayak A Day

A few months back, I purchase several kayaks and open Yelapa Kayak Rentals. Having "yakked" on the Central Coast of California, I jumped at the chance to return to an activity I loved and to re-acquire the svelte body which results. I'll keep you posted on the latter.

My coffee pot beeps at 7:30 a.m. Nikki eats her kibble; I enjoy half a *pan dulce* (Mexican sweet bread) with a mug of rich coffee. Crystal skies replace earlier clouds. I dash down stairs and head for my "yaks." Within five minutes, I launch into Yelapa Bay. Dorsal fins crease the surface as a pod of young dolphins hunts for breakfast. The bay is calm, unlike yesterday when swells crashed against house-sized boulders and sent sea mist to the tree line. I near the Lagunita Pier beginning the final corner on my loop (Do loops have corners?) and paddle back toward home base. Recent rains force the River Tuito bank-to-bank before it surges into the bay. Ocean swells smash against river current. The sight and sound define nature.

The Tuito, perhaps a hundred feet across, courses with silt. Its flow originates from summer storms over *Cabo Corrientes*, our county. I am surrounded by a setting reminiscent of the great Amazon. Shorelines offer refuge to avian waders, tree sitters, high fliers and insect snatchers. Squadrons of ducks scatter. A sandbar gently halts my progress. Dislodging is easy; the bow pivots and I, along with the river, flow back toward the bay.

Rituals

Sunday contains more rituals than any other day. It starts with sleeping in late, pancakes, waffles, brunch out-BC (before children), reading bits of the Sunday paper, or attending church. Afternoon rituals bring phone calls to friends, meal with the extended family and sports on the TV. Evening rituals close out the day by preparing for work or school, a return to church, more sports on the TV, or perhaps some type of intellectual engagement.

In Yelapa, my morning begins with a stretch. The mosquito netting separates.

Two steps later Nikki is at my side wiggling a full-body "Good Morning." She eats and drinks. I sip a mug of bold coffee (coincidentally named Memo's) and head to the couch. My day unfolds, not with the passage of time, but with a sequence of events. There is a difference! Shadows on the mountains retreat. The lone cloud vanishes upriver. *Pangueros* ply their morning trade. Ah, but today is Sunday, right? That means *birria* at Ray's Place.

Seductive Mexican music beckons. I am Odysseus passing the Sirens; I submit. I enter and smile to all. I plunk at my usual table, usual chair. The ritual unfolds; my order ever constant: three tacos, one consommé, and a Bloody Maria. A spider, resembling a leaf fragment creeps into focus. It undertakes the ritual of web building, reproducing angle after angle on its journey, a flawless work-in-progress. I remain mesmerized until jolted by Alexa who brings my order.

Three double-plied tortillas with *birria* meat fill my plate. Four small bowls containing cut limes, chopped onions and diced cilantro, a green guacamole-based salsa and a red jalapeño-based salsa await. Let the ritual begin. I sprinkle onions into each taco;

repeat with cilantro. The guacamole salsa is dribbled liberally with any remainder added to the consommé. The red salsa must be surgically applied. Lastly, lime juice drips into each taco; this is science folks. The sirens wail; I submit. The first bite forces both eyes to roll while a guttural "mmmmmmm" escapes.

I push back from the table, yet there is my tiny companion. It remains at the exact point where my gaze left it earlier. Was it absorbed in my ritual? We share a good bye. *Que tenga buen dia.* (Have a good day

Yelapa Bound

A neighbor suggests that once you arrive in Yelapa, you turn your watch back thirty years. I urge you to be more radical. While awaiting the water taxi departing Los Muertos Pier, remove all gizmos which track time (watch, cell phone, sun dial, etc.) and stow them securely until the evening prior to your departure. During your stay adopt the mantra: the sun alerts you to the arrival of the morning or its absence to the onset of night; your stomach communicates when it requires sustenance; and your throat advises you when it desires refreshment. What else is there? The only activity which is remotely choreographed by time is the water taxi schedule. I removed my watch a year ago and don it only during my return to *Gringolandia* (USA).

"A" type personalities research all lodging opportunities, restaurants, and activities; visit, re-visit and print reviews from TripAdvisor and even, oh please tell me not, purchase the Yelapa movie (Which Way, Por Favor?). Some venture here, especially those from the Portland area, on the recommendation of a friend, a hair-dresser, or a travel agent. Our last trekkers are the rugged types. They schlep huge containers on their backs. Leap off the water taxi at the main beach and in five minutes are consuming the good, albeit basic, life in the shadow of a pitched techno-tent. Over the next few hours, each group will develop diverse expectations. No research prepares you for the sound of the wind blowing through the Parthenon, or the scent inside the Sistine Chapel or the rush you feel when your water taxi captain forces the throttle forward. The less bound you are by expectations, the greater your experience. Just a thought.

Let's talk about packing your bag. Hopefully, your stay in Yelapa is at least three days. Pack three tops, three pair of under-alls, one pair of khaki shorts, one swim suit, a pair of flip-flops dedicated for inside only, and a pair of Teva-type sandals for outside only. You need sunblock (30 SPF) and Deet laden insect spray. This list is gender neutral. If you're fortunate to stay a week or more, simply add one to each of the items listed. Either hand wash or drop it off early morning at Ley's Laundry for same day pick-up. If you bring a laptop with you, include a medium sized plastic bag in the carrier. Cover the case prior to departing on the water taxi. (Tip: None of the locals care about how fabulous you appear, only that you appear appropriately.)

While a few restaurants accept credit/debit cards, cash is your best bet. There are ATMs (cajeras automaticas) all over Puerto Vallarta including at the airport. Exchange rates approximate 13:1, 1300 pesos equal $100 USD. Many locals accept US$s at a rate of 10:1 to keep the math easy. (i.e. $10 US equals 100 pesos). In advance, alert your credit/debit card company that you will be traveling in Mexico. This will avoid generating a fraud alert and lock out on your card. An event which can take days to unwind and untold international cell phone charges. I speak from experience.

Yelapa is a village of working people. The majority labors to give you, their guest, the most gracious experience possible. The village is not a high end, all-inclusive resort. Locals will greet you with their eyes, and respond with a smile to any utterance resembling *"hola"* or *"buenos dias."* Leave your "other world" behind, after all, it is Yelapa you traveled to experience, right?

Gringolandia (November)

Place A is neither better nor worse than place B. It simply possesses its own litany of descriptors. I have the option to choose which descriptors suit me. Both my wife and I, independently, spent decades in the "burbs" of Los Angeles as young professionals with families. Three cosmic events brought us to Yelapa: 1) adult children, 2) the advent of cheap airfares, and 3) HGTV's introduction of weekly episodes of House Hunter's International. By now Diana and I had found each other (what a difference a spouse makes). Each adventure, whether domestic or foreign, invited the question "Could we do this?" We stopped judging a location and searched for its descriptors.

Over the past year, we have grown to love Yelapa. The oppressive heat and humidity have subsided; the village is spruced and aromas flood even the most narrow of pathways. We are home.

"Thar she blows"

Each Fall, humpback whales gather in Banderas Bay. They feed, cavort, breach, and finally females signal their availability via thunderous fin slapping on the surface of the water. It is one of many natural spectacles. Rumor has it that the spiciness of Mexican krill inflames the giant mammalian libido.

November 1st is the official Ok to Start Sighting Whales Day. Necks crane and eyes strain for a telltale spouting. For two weeks, the majority of us experience stiff necks and eye fatigue.

Diana and I sip morning coffee while peering out our picture window. Pulses pound as we watch one, then two, ultimately three pods of dolphins glide into the bay. They are here for one reason and it is not to sun bathe. Geysers of small fish erupt only to fall into the open mouths of pursuers. Their bellies full, these denizens depart with grace. We smile.

Half-way through a refill, I hear a loud "wop." Two, and later an entire school, of adolescent manta rays arrive. The noise is created by these black and white sea wings breaching into the air and then landing belly-flop style. Two rays repeat the acrobatics. The school cruises the beach front as if to take a victory lap before departing. We chortle.

Nikki, our English Shepherd, heads for the front door. We walk to a location fifty paces away. We barely arrive when Diana hollers "Memo, there's a whale in the bay." What am I to do? Nikki satisfies her needs and we return to *Casa Azul*. Diana is past jubilant and approaching giddy. She recounts every detail; the doubting of what she saw; the gentle rolling of their characteristic dorsal areas and ultimately the fluted tail straight up signaling descent. The dolphins and manta rays were the warm-up acts.

Californians stare into their morning commute while New Yorkers gaze at a second cup of java. Diana and I sigh, smile and kiss. It is a great day to be Yelapan!

Mexican Food

Erase all prior perceptions regarding Mexican Food. Local palate pleasing purveyances grant the diner an unbridled partaking of perfected family recipes (I majored in alliteration in college). The blend of a potent salsa, the nuances of a marinade, and the merging of tastes captured from a seasoned grill are staples defining Mexican meal preparation. It just never stops.

By all means scan my comments on TripAdvisor regarding restaurants in Yelapa. After your visit, post your own. In our village, TripAdvisor is a powerful tool for attracting visitors, and provides for healthy competition among the participants.

Here are a few comments on our favorite spots (in alphabetical order):

Café Bahia
Located at the base of the town pier, Susan Pasko creates egg dishes for breakfast and healthy sandwiches for lunch. All ingredients are fresh to the point that the herbs and spices are plucked from her garden that morning. Produce is washed with microdyn and only purified water is used. Her restaurant is a focal point for the ex-pat community.

El Manguito
Located upriver, across the bridge; a right turn will take you past the elementary school. The restaurant will be on your right. If you are traveling from Hotel Lagunita just follow your feet up the river path. The owners, Luis and Angelica Castillon, offer an extensive menu from fresh fish to traditional enchiladas and *chile rellenos.* Their forte is shrimp in mango, coconut, papaya, garlic, or tequila sauce.

Pollo Bollo

Situated on the pathway heading out to The Point, this restaurant is known for its substantial portions. A favorite with visitors remains the Bar-B-Q half chicken. My personal favorite is the mixed *fajitas*. All meat and foul are marinated before grilling. The nuanced flavors arising from fresh shallots, green peppers and tomatoes linger on your palate.

Ray's Place

Ray, Violeta, Alexa and their assistant, Martina, create the greatest meals in Yelapa. Each order is made individually which requires more time. Mixed brochettes, bacon wrapped shrimp, *arrachera* steak and *pollo catalina* are but a few of the dozen entrees. Ray opens for breakfast (coffee, smoothies, and omelets) and lunch (tacos, Martina's enchiladas, and more) and dinner. This year will see additional vegetarian offerings. Ray is a master of libation creation and customer service, Violeta, his wife, and Martina support him with food preparation associated with a five star restaurant. Their daughter, Alexa, possesses the most beautiful smile in all Yelapa. If you are famished, try the plate-sized hamburger. It is the finest I have ever tasted and available in beef, chicken or portobello mushroom versions. Should your stay overlap a Sunday morning, a return for *birria* is a must. Word of advice--

go early (9:30 am) as this is a local ritual. The actual preparation begins at 4 a.m. and the supply is exhausted by 11:30.

Buen Provecho! (that's Spanish for *bon a petit*)

Bloggers Block

Just returned from Sunday *birria* at Ray's Place. My belly is full and my thirst is quenched. Life is good.......right up to the point that I sense my mind is void of any clue for this week's blog. So what now? I react in the manner males have done for centuries, ... I sit and ponder. I ponder my most recent insect bite; I ponder the water line on the rocks across the bay; I ponder Nikki's belly when I rub it; I even ponder my belly. Then suddenly an errant thought descends into the transom of my mind------advance to the kitchen-----open the refrigerator----remove a *Pacifico*, plunk your rump on the couch and await inspiration. . . Alas, it works every time!

We live at the top of a four story concrete building. *Casa Azul* is a spacious *casita* with an entryway, kitchen, tiled bathroom, living/dining area and two large bedrooms. The north-facing wall supports five-foot tall windows across its span of twelve feet. The vista reveals the entirety of the main beach and extends into the Bay of Banderas. Every water taxi, *panga*, kayak, log, beach towel, reclining lounge, dog, ice chest or bare chest is observable. It becomes a sixty square foot big screen. Diana and I lose hours gazing in amusement.

As I write this, one of our neighbors is testing a new wing with his motor-assisted, parasail. While the small motor spews noises akin to a Tim Allen blender, the aerial acrobatics mitigate my irritation. He sways, ascends nearly vertically, kills the motor and pilots around the bay. Visitors on the beach lust for such freedom; dogs chase the shadow to bark at some perceived flying threat. He executes a return to the sandy beach, observers applaud; he smiles and responds to their polite inquiries.

Sunday is family day in Yelapa. Youth frolic in whatever surf splashes over them. Teenage boys appear with boogie boards in tow. They pass hours shouting, riding and tumbling in the swells. Shadows announce the arrival of evening, families re-group; the young males scan the horizon for one last wave set; the beach empties. Paradise invites engagement and immersion.

Olympiad   (December)

I lived in the Los Angeles basin during the

1984 Summer Olympics. I witnessed the traveling torch and watched a soccer (*futbol*) match in the Rose Bowl. That was thirty years ago. I recall the awe of the torch passing. The sound of the runner's shoes on the track, the visual created by the unitary arm-torch-flame, the labored breathing as he strove to conceal any sign of fatigue; it is a moment remembered.

In an earlier post, I wrote that the locals spruce up their stores, lodging spaces, restaurants, water taxi, beach furniture and each other. Why? You've forgotten already! The reason for this heightened state of activity is the seasonal arrival of the world's tourists. Consider it akin to delivering the torch or perhaps the running of the bulls in Pamplona, Spain. Adjust the metaphor to reflect less bulls but running none-the-less. Locals acknowledge that for six months, there is indeed a lot of bull in town. We are an accepting people.

November 1; the temperatures remain high, the humidity is even higher; incoming water taxi passengers increase; however, visitors spend the day and depart.

November 15; the temperatures remain high, the humidity has dropped to the point of paralleling the temperatures (good news); water taxi traffic increases but lodging and restaurant occupancy remains low.

Thanksgiving Day; temperatures drop a few degrees taking the humidity with it. Virtually all ex-pats and long-term seasonal visitors meet and greet over turkey, smashed potatoes and margaritas. Only a few bulls walk the streets.

December 1; temperatures drop into the high 70s F with humidity falling into the mid-50s. Nights are cool, requiring a cover. The early daylight hours are drop-dead gorgeous. A breeze continues through mid-morning. Whale sightings occur. Incoming and departing water taxi are filled to the gunnels-----yet where are the balance of the bulls? Merchants meet you with their eyes; inquisitive frowns crease their foreheads. Lodging managers escort a couple to their room, then shrug as the balance of their accommodations remain vacant. We are a village on edge.

Yet another metaphor to punctuate the point; consider Disneyland poised for the opening bell. One day, the gatekeeper ambles forward to fling open the entrance to the Magic Kingdom and ------------no cars occupy the parking lot. Now, Yelapa is not the Magic Kingdom and fortunately we are without parking lots and vehicles. Diana and I expect the arrival of three friends within two weeks. Hopefully, everyone else does as well. If not, there will be untold meals/beverages not consumed; sunrises/sunsets missed; whales/dolphins/manta rays not cited; etc. etc. etc. Come on folks, I know you have four days of vacation time tucked away. Yelapa awaits you!!!

Yelapan Healthcare

Those who travel seek new sites, experience new people and consume new delicacies. Never do we consider the potential of a medical event. If you are planted in a high-rise hotel in a major city, you call the front desk and the scene plays out from there. What if you are located in a remote village forty minutes by water taxi from Puerto Vallarta?

Ok, say you become ill, scrape your foot, or the guy forgets his vacation "meds" and you are in PV, you're covered. What happens if you are staying in Yelapa? Here's what you can expect. Yelapa is home to a beautiful, well-staffed (two doctors and a nurse) health clinic. Check out their Face Book page: *Centro de Salud Yelapa.*

Two American friends of mine seek care at the clinic. Their needs are met efficiently and professionally and NO CHARGES are assessed. In each case, the individuals make a contribution equal to what an out of pocket office call costs in the States. If a major medical situation arises, the clinic stabilizes the patient and arranges transport to Puerto Vallarta. There is a designated emergency *panga* for such situations. We meet and greet our doctors by their first names. They are a valued and honored part of our community. (An expanded discussion of medical services in Puerto Vallarta appears in the section Retiring in Yelapa)

A word about scorpions; although one typically thinks of this insect's habitat as the desert, it also lives here. It is non-aggressive and prefers dark, damp surroundings. However, when cornered or provoked, it will defend itself. Remember, it's the back end that you need to watch. Each morning shake out your shoes, clothing, backpacks, or anything that might afford overnight lodging. As part of the community health plan, locals in each of the four colonies of Yelapa can administer an anti-venom injection 24/7.

You arrive in Yelapa to rest, relax, eat, drink and enjoy. Remember the "think" part also.

Memo's Favorites

I scan my calendar and ponder the manifest blessings bestowed upon me these past months. GAG! This is not a moment for obtuse reflection; it is an instant to move forward. *VIVA!* The mere act of reflection raises my paranoia filter. Does anyone else harbor the concern that they might look rearward to reflect and see nothing but the reflection their rear?

Instead, I offer gifts. These are my selections and I am gifting them to you, my readers, to relish for the coming year.

Memo's Favorites   2012

Best cup of Coffee	Café Bahia
Cheapest beer on La Playa	Domingo's
Best Margarita/Restaurant	Ray's Place
Best Shrimp Dinner	El Manguito
Best Attraction	Town Waterfall
Best Guide–fishing	Okley Excursions
Best Kayak Rental	Yelapa Kayak Rentals
Best Electronic Bargain	TelCel Cellphone

Our pueblo offers much to all visitors. There are food and beverage purveyors galore, physical activities and comfortable lodging. However, if your "travels" to Yelapa include only my blog, online videos or a travel book from the library, then rest assured a warm *"hola"* awaits you.

Loose Ends

Two months ago the Yelapa Memo blog began. The twelve postings speak to nature and kayaking, food and frolic, local culture and rituals, plus embracing a new point of view.

One post requires an update (Yelapa Health Clinic). Recently, I required care. Without engaging in details, let's just say that I was bitten during the night by a venomous spider. The next morning my right hand resembles a catcher's mitt, my right eye is swollen shut and my ears could audition for the remake of Dumbo. I react in the manner that males do and postpone seeking medical attention for twenty-four hours. It is the wrong decision. The following morning, off to the clinic I go. I spend twenty minutes with the doctor watching him attempt to mask his shock. He hooks up an IV and I experience the first of three anti-venoms necessary to combat the toxin. Since our local clinic does not possess the additional two, I must depart for Puerto Vallarta and report to the Regional Hospital. Cost to me at the Yelapa Clinic = $0. We arrive at the hospital and over the ensuing nine hours (Did I mention this occurs on Diana's Birthday?) another IV is connected and I receive the remaining anti-venoms. At 1:00 a.m., we depart. Cost to me at the Regional Hospital = 200 pesos ($16 USD). I continue to mend thanks to all. *Gracias a todos.*

Without structuring this post as a set of hopes for the new year, I want to identify two important issues: good health and cherished friends. My challenge to you is simple: 1) add an event to your routine which is health based, and 2) commit to making at least one new friend.

Prospero Año Nuevo!

"i-s-h"   (January)

There are countless prefixes and suffixes in English, yet none more easily transitions into Spanish than "ish." In English, the intended meaning relates to ancestry; (e.g. "English," "Spanish," " Polish"). In Spanish, a much less complicated language, the connection is clear, concise and instantly understandable. It relates to the future arrival of an undefined instant in time. Work with me.

Everything enters and departs Yelapa via *panga*. People, dogs, bottled water, beer, vegetables, dry goods, building materials and medical supplies all arrive; are consumed; and depart in some form via boat. Now in order to support a village of twelve hundred men, women, children, dogs, horses and mules, a highly sophisticated scheduling infrastructure must be in place, right? Nope! All life in Yelapa adheres to the "ish" principle. If you travel to Puerto Vallarta tomorrow, you choose the *panga* departing from the town pier 8:30 ish. It simply means that the *panga* will depart within the time span defined by the first part of the expression. In this case, 8 refers to an hour; as long as the *panga* departs within an hour of 8:30, it is on time.

Perhaps additional examples might help. One day each week Sammy ferries a *panga* full of scrap metal to PV. The word circulates that he is departing Thursday; Thursday relates to the identification of a day. He could actually depart Thursday or Friday and still be considered to have kept his original schedule. Get it? Ok, one more: last week, I run into Nacho, the plumber. We discuss a repair. He responds that he would be happy to stop by the following week. Question: What actual period of time does Nacho have to appear and still honor his original promise? Answer: Two weeks!

Travel Hint: Adopt the concept of "ish" when traveling to rural anywhere. Practice in advance of your departure. Randomly remove a device from your person which tracks the actual day/month/date/year/hour/nano-second. Start off slowly, perhaps ten-one minute repetitions. Let me know how it goes.

Weekly News

Sunshine in Yelapa is a natural resource. Its absence is an ill omen. Last week a storm moves in and delivers two afternoons of rain. We then enjoy three spectacular sun-filled days. Shopkeepers grin, children sing *"hola"* to all who pass and the local clutch of canines smiles as they nap in patches of brightness. Then BAM!!! We are cast into three days of clouds and mist. Shopkeepers snarl, children hang their heads while babies and dogs howl as if to bemoan some lost companion. Occurrences of SAD (Seasonal Affective Disorder) approach epidemic status requiring the local clinic to provide emergency housing for husbands who feel their lives are at risk should they return home to their spouses. We are a village in turmoil.

In perhaps an unrelated incident, one of our local water taxi encounters a visiting hump-back whale. Apparently the thirty foot, multi-ton mammal breeches just as the taxi passes; causing a minor collision. Damage is sustained by the taxi resulting in it being towed back to Yelapa. No injuries are reported. Numerous attempts to contact the whale for comment prove unsuccessful.

Sunday Evening

Dusk descends on our village. The Great Frigate birds, that dominate the skies since early morning, separate and scatter. Common vultures cease their circling and select palm trees to house their hulks. Snowy Egrets, which devote their day to strutting on the beach, amass to roost up river. For the next hour, the *playa* is populated by fishermen, their sons, and their son's sons spinning and casting hand lines into the surf. It is the essence of tranquility.

The jungle abounds with vibrancy. It also is home to death and recycling. Our village experiences two deaths this week. Both are natives whose ages reach into the four score range. As is the local ritual, once the embalmed body returns from Puerto Vallarta, family and friends station a twenty-four hour vigil to afford "the departed" protection from evil spirits. The next morning, the coffin is carried by four men to the cemetery. The balance of the day passes in celebration of the deceased's life.

The whale collisions continue to render our taxi drivers anxious. Two additional incidences result in the loss of a motor and people in the water. No explanation surfaces for this behavior. In response, there is an increase in the number of individuals making the sign of the cross as well as the wearing of life vests. It never hurts to double down on both religious and secular fronts.

Lastly, a town cleanup is launched today. In observation of which, I descend to the *Playita* and scour the entire beach from in front of my "office" all the way past the Yacht Club.

Clouds caress the ridgelines surrounding our village. A glow stretches across the bay silhouetting visitors returning from their evening repast. Juanito-the son; Juan-the father and Don Juan the grand-father approach their abode, clean the fish and deliver it for cooking. This trio will retrace their steps in the morning to welcome the first rays of the sun and accept whatever bounty the sea surrenders. We are a pueblo at rest.

Buenas noches!

Tips/Tipping

Visitors frequently ask "When do I tip, and how much should I tip?" Some countries calculate a gratuity and include it on the tab. As long as you are aware the calculation exists, then it becomes a no-brainer; you pay the largest amount on the bill. Mexico is not one of those countries. Tipping guidelines are similar to those in the States (e.g. 10%-15%).

Unlike in the States, wait staff do not receive a minimum wage. Here in Yelapa, tips are the ONLY earnings received by waiters, luggage handlers, guides and helpers in general. So my solution to the "how much" issue is driven by what was the value to me of the service performed. Would I pay someone 10 pesos for carrying a 5 gallon bottle of water up two flights of stairs? You bet! Would I offer a baggage handler 50 pesos for pushing suitcases uphill in a wheelbarrow? In a heartbeat! Would I tip a waiter 20% for an excellent meal with superb service? Done! This approach mirrors what I pay stateside.

Confusion or awkward moments arise when you pay for a specific service (e.g. fishing trip, horseback ride, a guide for a specific period of time/destination) and the agreed upon service at the agreed upon price is completed; are you then expected to offer a tip? This should be totally discretionary. If the level of service provided was excellent, then certainly any tip you feel appropriate is appreciated. Keep in mind that you may wish to return to this individual and rest assured, he will remember your earlier generosity.

A word of caution: problems can arise innocently (or ignorantly) when the traveler is unfamiliar with the appearance/denomination/value of the foreign currency. We've all mused at how another country's currency reminds us of Monopoly money only to experience at the end of the day that the $500 US dollars we just exchanged has evaporated. Currency in Mexico is a distinct color and size for each denomination (20, 50, 100, 200, 500, 1000). Learn the appearance and value ($US) of the various bills. Certainly the adage of "time is money" is apropos. Spend some time with yours; you'll enjoy it longer.

So much to do; so little time (February)

It's Sunday morning; Diana and I return from our *birria* at Ray's Place. The weather is spectacular. Temps range from the high 70s to low 80s. Sunday is family day in Yelapa. Some motor slowly in their *pangas* as the men/boys drag or toss hand lines while the ladies/girls adorn a bench. Others rent kayaks and traverse the bay. Even the local canines dial back a notch. Their movements alternate between short stints in the sun to longer stints burrowed into shady, damp sand. A few visitors cue up to "fly" the bay while suspended by parachute. Church bells toll, beckoning the faithful. This same group re-emerges within the hour; collects stray family members; fills an ice chest then heads for the beach.

Over the past several days, I observe one chap who is a bit of a conundrum. Each day from 2:00 p.m. until 6:00 p.m. this elderly gent crisscrosses the beach wagging a metal detector. This lone soul trudges for hours seemingly drawn by the unknown, past the unaware or more likely the unbelieving. I have several theories as to his *raison de etre*. They are, in order of likelihood:

1) the gadget, a pulse induction metal detector, is given to him by one of his adult children. Upon hearing of his pending travels to Yelapa, they decide that this might be a means of activating an otherwise sedentary patriarch.
Or
2) the PIMD is a gift from his wife of fifty-five years who knows that due to her husband's fading auditory capacity, any attempt to communicate with him on the beach with the surf in the background is futile. In this fashion he is busy for countless hours while wearing earphones which preclude him from hearing anything at all;
Or
3) Upon learning that a three week Mexican Riviera vacation is booked by his wife, he immediately seeks advice from his neighbor who discusses the benefits of traveling with a PIMD: 1) placing distance between yourself and any family members with whom you are required to travel; 2) being able to approach bikini clad women in a non-threatening manner; 3) disappearing down paths/walkways

for hours and returning well after any accompanying grand children are placed into bed. The good neighbor even suggests that batteries are not required to achieve any of the above and simply add weight.

I'll keep you posted.

Water Taxi

Yelapa is only accessible by water taxi departing Puerto Vallarta or Boca de Tomatlan. During the dry season, there is FWD access from El Tuito to the top of the ridge above our village. The near two hour trek is used primarily for the delivery of building materials. The water taxi is our lifeline to the outside world; our public shuttle.

The schedule during the high season (November thru April) offers thirteen daily departures to Boca; seven continue on to Vallarta. Service commences at 7:45am-ish and continues almost hourly until 6:00pm-ish. Bear in mind that time in Yelapa is approximate. Service operates daily, regardless of sea or weather conditions. While all water taxi have overhead awnings, little protection is afforded from horizontal winds bearing sea mist or rain. Generally the rides are uneventful. Locals are greeted by name as they board. People even say "thank you" to the Captain upon departure. Older people are respectfully assisted into and out of the taxi, while packages are stored and then retrieved at the destination. Captains frequently return to a pier to pick up tardy travelers.

There are two loosely organized driver groups, referred to as *cooperativos*. They provide all passengers assurance that the taxi is safe (life jackets are on board) and that the vessel is seaworthy. Do mechanical breakdowns occur? Of course. Is there the odd occasion when the driver miscalculates his remaining fuel? Yes. But these are rare. The drivers are local men who grew up, in and around the sea. They received training from a father, uncle or older brother. During a new moon/full moon the tides and sea swells are the most extreme, their seamanship capabilities are tested. They must be able to "decode" the sea, calculate wave height, swell timing, and recall the location of shallow rocks while adjusting their speed and heading to maximize passenger comfort. Most are masters of their trade.

Buying taxi tickets whether at Los Muertos Pier or Boca de Tomatlan may create an awkward moment for the unknowing traveler. Accept the fact that as you head down the street to either of the piers, you are a "marked" traveler. You will be asked repeatedly if you are traveling to Yelapa. Just lie and say "no." That's right, you need to lie. The taxi cooperatives engage vendors to sell tickets at both departure points. If you buy a ticket, it will identify passage on that particular coop's group of boats; it is not transferrable. This means that your return voyage will be limited to that coop's taxi and travel times. Here's what we do. When approached to buy a ticket, we shake our heads and proceed to the end of the pier. We know when the next taxi is departing. When the taxi arrives, you simply board. You may be asked to pay prior to getting on the boat, that's ok. Then the timing of your return is in no way limited. Once you board the taxi, grab the overhead center support pole for stability and walk on the benches. Drop down when you reach your desired spot.

Tip: Move as far to the rear of the taxi as possible and then sit in the center of the bench. These two items will assure you experience the most comfortable ride possible.

Local News: Susan Pasko, Café Bahia, has set up a new FaceBook open access page entitled "Yelapa Visitors." It is intended to be a hub for new and repeat visitors alike. Check it out, and see what is happening that day or in the week ahead. It features a current Water Taxi Schedule

A Proper Greeting

I love the seductive language of Mexico. It is composed of long vowels and soft consonants. Not only is it pleasant to hear spoken or sung, it is inviting to learn. The language enjoys an underlying repetitive structure which eludes my native English.

Eye contact serves as a universal invitation to engage. No eye contact between approaching individuals; no communication sought. It's an issue of comfort.

The Spanish language offers several simple options:

"Hola"
This is the greeting extended by all, children and adults. It requires minimal response, either in-kind or with a simple nod of the head joined by eye contact.

"Hola amigo"
This greeting defines the first step up the ladder of friendship. It is issued by/to someone that you recognize from an earlier encounter. You need not know the individual's name.

"Hola mi amigo"
Yet another rung up the ladder, this greeting comes into play when you interact

with an individual yet again. Perhaps they assisted you with your luggage; perhaps they are a waiter at a restaurant you visited more than once; perhaps they are a *panguero* (*panga* owner) you helped on the beach.

"Hola, buenos dias/buenas tardes/buenas noches"

At the top of our greeting hierarchy, we introduce respect. *"Hola"* followed by the appropriate greeting of the day engages someone your senior or when entering any space occupied by numerous adults (e.g. market, home, a bench on the pier, etc.).

Shaking hands is not observed in Yelapa, except between ex-pats. If/when you are accepted by the locals as a reasonable American, you may be invited to share in the ritual of the hand bump. This is a status few achieve.

Yelapans are a welcoming people. They understand that guests provide financial support during the high season and fund their reserves during the five months of oppressive heat. Meet them, greet them. You now possess a ten-word vocabulary to enhance your Yelapa experience. *Buenas suerte!*

Farmers Market in Puerto Vallarta

Diana and I descend our stairs and trek to

the pier. We arrive and head out to the approaching taxi. After greeting the captain and his helper, plus half a dozen familiar faces, we cross Banderas Bay. I close my eyes and float along rocking-horse style to the rhythm of the sea. Less frequent travelers oooh and aaah at the variety of fauna and flora, point and gasp at passing dolphins, whales or manta-rays and giggle as the swells smack the boat's bottom. The mood is upbeat.

Everyone departs the water taxi at Los Muertos Pier. Exiting the *panga* requires caution. We bid *"buenos dias"* to our travel mates. Saturday in Puerto Vallarta's Romantic Zone is busy. The restaurants are full and lines form in front of the ATMs as visitors fill their pockets with *pesos* to spend at the Farmers Market.

We head up Basilio Badillo Street to a favorite breakfast stop, The Pancake House, which is not related to IHOP although it exhibits identical colors on the sign. Several cups of coffee compliment two large plates of breakfast. We depart to mingle with the masses. One can purchase foodstuffs, soaps, apparel, jewelry, flutes, and massage services. The atmosphere is electric.

Time passes quickly; the eleven o'clock hour approaches. We separate; Diana continues shopping while I head up one block to the dentist's office to acquire a pair of new fillings. Nothing forces me to my emotional knees faster than the sight/sound of a high-speed dental drill. Shortly after our arrival in Yelapa, we read about a group of dental professionals who are opening an office in the *Zona Romantica.* All the office staff and practitioners are bilingual. The practice, Just Smiles, (www.justsmiles.com.mx/) serves the dental needs of PV ex-pats as well as the visiting English speaking public. Appointments are generally available within twenty-four hours and ALL work is performed by dentists. The first time Diana and I visit, our teeth are cleaned by an orthodontist. The equipment reflects the latest in technology and the facilities are spotless.

Let's return to my two cavities. I am greeted and invited upstairs by my dentist. She is a petite, lean, dental machine. Above her cabinet, I spy a pair of red boxing gloves. I nervously inquire if that's what she uses instead of Novocain. She smiles tolerantly, and responds that she boxes as a form of exercise. I recoil and promise to behave. She plies her profession and after a while states that I am free to go. Then, almost as an aside, she turns to me and in perfect English tells me that she actually did three fillings. There will be no additional charge since she only discussed two in my earlier visit. I reach for the counter to steady myself. We smile warmly at each other and I descend the stairs to pay my bill. The receptionist prints my receipt and informs me that today's visit will cost $56 USD. I turn with a look of shock toward Diana. The following words stumble across my lips, "That was great." She shakes her head.

Two Gentlemen of Yelapa   (March)

Sunday morning arrives in Yelapa. A pair of water taxi rest on the beach awaiting a spiff before returning to service. Blue skies stretch the entirety of Banderas Bay. Paradise unfolds. And yes, Diana and I have just returned from *birria* at Ray's Place.

There are two gentlemen who help define Yelapa. The first is Mario, the popsicle vendor. He commutes daily from Puerto Vallarta. Mario totes two coolers customized by layers of duct tape. Arriving mid-morning, he treks from the town pier to the playa where he departs 2:30pm-ish. He is the most sought after vendor in town. One day Diana and her friend, Erin, are catching some tan time on the *playa*. Half way down the beach a gathering grows. They approach, the sounds of gleeful children, swooning women and cursing men are discernible. At the epicenter is Mario with his twin coolers. Diana and Erin sprint to the spot arriving just in time to acquire the last two treasures. The flavor is irrelevant, it is the shear possession of the popsicle which matters. Just for the record, Mario offers five flavors: chocolate chip, butter pecan, strawberry, coconut, and lime. All include a core of rich, (forget about milk fat for a moment), yellow vanilla ice cream. On a warm day, locals buy them in pairs. The first disappears and sets the stage for the second one to linger slowly. Children "read" a popsicle not unlike their fathers "read" the sea. They know where and when to bite just in advance of any portion melting and dripping onto the sand. This is an evolutionary adaptation supported by generations of popsicle trials.

Our second chap is Pancho, the pharmacist. He arrived in Yelapa around the first of the year and rents a small space at street level in the building in which Diana and I live. His store hours are 9ish-6ish daily. A personal cell number appears on his overhead sign. I witness his returning as late as 11:30pm as he attends to a local or a visitor in need. Over the past two months, his business increases. Virtually all our ex-pats now deal with him on their medications. He occupies a white plastic chair strategically positioned in the center of his entryway. Daily, a growing band of children are found at his feet reading from a book, telling a story or just sharing some intricate aspect of their lives. He smiles to each of them. He is their Pied Piper, a gentle, peaceful man.

There are roughly twelve hundred stories in the village of Yelapa. I have presented but two. Over the coming weeks I will acquaint you with others.

Update (six months later)

I have just learned that my good friend and great human being, Francisco Brindis Samos (Pancho) died last night in Puerto Vallarta. Apparently, he experienced a spike in blood pressure that ruptured an aneurism in his brain. He was transported by *panga* to Puerto Vallarta, where he died two days later.

He gave selflessly to all, volunteered his dental skills to the village of Pizota. He established a much needed pharmacy here in Yelapa so that those who could not travel to Vallarta could have necessary medication. He was 53 years of age. Diana, Nikki and I will miss him. RIP *Mi Amigo*.

Yelapa Rediscovered

Early morning, I receive an e-message from Patrick, a sometimes Yelapan, and reluctant resident of Chicago. He states that two friends will be visiting. I assure him they will be treated well. Brad and Dan arrive at the town pier. While the morning remains overcast; they revel as the mid-day temperatures approach 80 F. Their mid-western turf currently "enjoys" its third snow storm of the season. Chicago mid-day highs will flirt with the freezing mark.

The pair is easy to spot as they depart the water taxi. Like other visitors to Mexico, they spend the first day or two lounging around the pool or at the beach only to acquire a tropical glow that remains over the balance of their stay. Spirits undaunted, they launch into discovery. Our first destination is the town waterfall. They chat about their crossing on the water taxi. We pause at the rosewood workshop and view the crafts of the Rodriguez family. We pass a display of necklaces, beads and handmade shawls. We stop, speak, and smile as the vendor details, in her best English, the time involved in creating the various crafts. We arrive at the falls. A few moments are dedicated to watching, listening and absorbing this serenely special site.

My guests retrace their steps; greeting oncoming traffic with a smile and an *"hola."* We reconnect with the main path. There are no street signs in Yelapa although most streets do possess names. These are long forgotten. Only the village elders recall such trivia. For the next three quarters of an hour,

our trio ambles along, stopping to investigate some plant or flower, or to glance between buildings to gain a bearing on the bay. Angelica beckons us to lunch at El Manguito. Resistance would be useless. Nourished and quenched we return to the path. There is a required stop at Patrick's house to "ooh and aah." Debbie, a friend and local massage therapist, is house-sitting and grants a tour.

The last leg of our journey summons. It is a half hour stroll from Patrick's house to the main beach. Ancient guanava trees create trellises where vines merge and shade abounds. Passing neighborhood stores, we approach one of the beachfront restaurants. We are ushered to a table, my guests enjoy a margarita; I, a *Pacifico*. Moments later I bid them *"adios."* As I return to *Casa Azul*, I realize that somehow/sometime I became muted to the beauty that surrounds me. It is reset today through sharing with others. Dan and Brad discover Yelapa with genuine appreciation through fresh eyes. Thank you, gentlemen for a most enjoyable day.

La Tortilla

The humble *tortilla* is Mexico's national bread. It is available from wheat flour which yields a smooth, pliable tortilla, or from corn flour which crafts a thicker less pliable counterpart. Edge to edge the standard tortilla is six inches. Larger models become *quesadillas* while smaller models double up to become small tacos. The larger fall into the category of specialty versions. Current pricing on a kilo (roughly twenty weighing 2.1 lbs.) of fresh *tortillas* is 9 *pesos* ($0.75 USD)

In Yelapa, there is a mechanized *tortillería*. A stainless steel, twelve-foot long machine blends ingredients and produces perfectly shaped warm corn *tortillas*. Work begins early so that one kilo bundles can be packed into coolers and delivered to the five markets throughout the village. The next round is deposited at the dozen restaurants and *taquerías*. This distribution system consists of one young man, on a nimble blue scooter. His progress throughout the village is announced by blasts from his horn. With required deliveries completed by mid-morning, he then cruises the streets marketing any remaining product to passersby or household clients. As before, his progress is punctuated with the scooter's brassy horn followed by *"llegaron tortillas."* (Tortillas are here.) By late morning, all product is sold and he retires. This cycle repeats seven days per week.

The combination of high humidity plus the absence of preservatives limits the shelf life of these life-sustaining disks. A paper wrapped kilo can be stored no more than two days. One way of extending the shelf life is to cut the *tortillas* into strips or triangles and fry them. This now alters the original product into chips/strips (*totopos/nachos*). These are placed alongside a bowl of salsa and disappear into mouths before dinner.

I recently attend a birthday party for the twelve-year old daughter of a good friend. The parents, both of whom are accomplished chefs, decide to produce a large caldron of spaghetti topped with meat and chili sauce. Sitting next to me is a gregarious five-year old. Understand that pasta is not something you're likely to see coming out of a Mexican kitchen. There is little, if any use of pasta in general. My diminutive table mate appears perplexed. Attempts to stab, spear or otherwise impale the spaghetti onto a fork prove futile. He pauses for a moment and then does what every kid in Mexico would do. He extracts a *tortilla* from a napkin-covered basket. The *tortilla* lays empty for a second before a fork scoots spaghetti up and onto it. My neighbor carefully rolls the tortilla, pinches it and transports it full of spaghetti and meat sauce directly into his tiny mouth. Dilemma solved.

The Taco Shop

The previous posting addressed the quintessential nature of the *tortilla*. Perhaps its most noble task is that of efficiently conveying fish or meat (beef, pork, tongue, chicken), beans, onions, chili peppers, shredded cabbage/lettuce and salsa from the plate into the mouth of the holder. We identify this delicacy as the *"taco."*

With a food so delicious, so portable and so easy to craft, it is no wonder that every village spawns sites where the hungry traveler can acquire just such sustenance. Any enterprising family is free to host a *taquería* (taco shop) by repurposing a vacant patio, an unscreened window or by simply placing plastic tables along the pathway. A grill sears the meat while a wooden press flattens the disc of fresh *maza* into the appropriate size; large for *quesadillas* and standard for *tacos*. The serving area is populated with all sorts of condiments. Lastly, in small bowls or squeeze bottles reside the various colors or temperaments of salsas. The client is free to add whatever they choose. The repast is paired with either cold beer, *jamaica* or *agua fresca* (freshly squeezed juice of the cantaloupe, guanava, mango, watermelon, papaya or pineapple). If hunger persists, order again.

A *taco* dinner for me and Diana typically plays out as follows: Memo: one *quesadilla*, two *tacos*, one *agua fresca;* Diana: something between two and four *tacos*, one *agua fresca*.

Total bill, less than 100 pesos ($8 USD) Do I have your attention?

Follow me on a *taquería* tour of Yelapa:

Señor Taco
Located up the river pathway just behind the restaurants on the main beach.

Janet's
Adjacent to the main path after you cross the bridge and head towards village center.

Ramona's
On your right side down the ramp which borders Yuri's Tienda.

Abuelos
Past Ramona's on the path between the casino and Isis Laundry. (This is also a full service restaurant.)

Olivia's
Across from the billiard hall.

Yolanda's
In the center of the village adjacent to the municipal steps.

Note: Hours of operation and nightly specials expand/contract as new shops open/close each season.

Cultural Note: Do not arrive in Mexico expecting a preformed, hard-shelled *taco* filled with ground meat, crumbled cheese, shredded lettuce and chopped tomatoes. This item only exists north of the border and is rumored to have been developed by a test kitchen in Salina, Kansas. The design flaws associated with this product were demonstrated in the movie *The Three Amigos.*

The Mexican *tortilla* is a marvel of ingenuity, beauty, simplicity and edibility all rolled into one, literally. *Buen Provecho!*

Easter Sunday   (April)

Sunday remains my favorite day; it's family day. This Sunday is mega-family day. As Easter approaches, incoming water taxi are filled with nationals visiting "country cousins." For every couple there are at least four children under the age of ten. Our village affords the "city cousins" the opportunity to freely roam the paths, play a limited number of primitive video games, romp on the beach or generally just hang out while large circles of parents, aunts/uncles, grandparents and other adults occupy plastic chairs on balconies, patios or along the main path. It is a festive time.

In front of my kayak platform sprawls a multi-generational family unit. Grandpa is fast asleep by a large boulder. Two couples occupy sand-filled beach towels evidencing frequent visitation by tiny feet. Coolers contain assorted snacks and beverages. The adults scan the water's edge less than twenty feet forward where a dozen jumping, splashing, running, squealing children frolic.

Down the beach resides a pair of young girls. They scheme, then swim out to a moored *panga.* It quickly becomes their headquarters. Other like-minded females follow populating the *panga* to near capacity. This concentration of femininity does not go unnoticed. A band of adolescent males storms the water, a la Braveheart. Fortunately, they wear appropriate attire. Girls scream, boys growl, bodies leap through the air. Pandemonium prevails! The damsels (the prey), flee to safe harbor from the warriors (the predators), and sequester a second *panga.* The young men, unwilling or unable to take prisoners, amass on the now vacant *panga* to ponder their next move. No discernible action occurs. The term "Mexican Standoff" defines the moment. One girl seizes the stage and leaps into the water, swimming toward yet a third *panga.* The ensuing moments find the two groups ultimately merging onto and off three *pangas.* There is continuous swimming, jumping and screaming. The boys, stricken with *machismo*, attempt acrobatics off one *panga.* They possess no idea as to why they must do this; it is a expression of some innate instinct.

Three couples in their mid-teens descend a ramp to lean against a stone wall. The *señoritas* are clad in snug semi-revealing tops complimented by short shorts or abbreviated cut-offs. The boys all wear the basic Yelapa uniform: t-shirt and board shorts. Each of the six has a cell phone in hand; they silently settle into their electronic world. Periodically, one glances up to exude disdain at the noise level of the groups occupying the water. The entire scene is reminiscent of a Carmen Lomas Garcia painting.

Dusk descends early in Yelapa due to a high ridge on the western border of the village. Following some silent signal, perhaps a group text, the teenagers arise to retrace their steps up the ramp. The remaining *panga* pirates sit astride individual benches. The clutch of little ones is retrieved, dried and returned to the home of their hosts. Tomorrow, hundreds of family members depart Yelapa for their city environs fatter and browner; affirmed that nothing beats a weekend in the country.

A Tribute

Perform an internet search for "Ghost Crab." In one tenth of a second, Google generates 1.4 million hits. You know what these little crustaceans are, right? They appear from countless caverns in the sand with one claw acting as a scooper/dumper. They proceed to pitch their load and race sideways back to their homes. Watching them becomes hypnotic, especially from my kayak platform on the *Playita*.

The ghost crabs are out, perhaps a hundred, all performing morning housekeeping duties. Endless teaspoon sized deposits of sand emerge to be transported a foot away and pitched. The crabs cross paths, pause for a second and disappear. Tiny eyes atop antenna style extensions afford visibility in all directions. Any sign of an intruder, each scampers sideways, propelled by eight legs independently engaging at warp speed. Within a nanosecond the *playita* is empty. This scenario plays out countless times. While I observe frequent canine attempts to pursue these creatures, I have yet to see said canine succeed. Nature protects these octopods.

The Old Man at the Sea

I arrive at the *playita*, plunk into my chair and scan the bay. A familiar face roams the beach. He is a mature gentleman, lean and bronzed by the Mexican sun. His routine rarely varies. A trash bag trails as he scours the upper beach for plastic bottles, paper wrappers, styro plates/cups or other discards. Our eyes meet, we nod and exchange an *"hola."* He commences to my right, follows a stone wall, veers to the left, crosses the creek and proceeds to the far corner of the beach. Stopping, stooping and plucking discards, he smiles as locals watch him with quiet amusement tempered by discomfort. Some speak, others ignore.

His route crosses the beach, morphs into the first curve of an oval and drops down to the water's edge. His bag floats awkwardly in the surf. More trash is plucked from sand and sea. He trudges along, resolute in his task. As the last curve of the oval closes, he pivots to appreciate the result. The *playita* returns to a pristine state. We nod to each other once again.

Of late, an additional task consumes his time. He enters the knee-high surf and scans the water for shell fragments. Once located, he extracts the piece and pitches it onto the sand. His progress is slow and methodical yet his practiced eye is no less capable of spotting a shell than an egret capturing a minnow. The number of shell fragments residing on the beach increases daily and now totals in the hundreds. This second task complete, he departs.

Later, I observe the following: a visiting

couple stroll the *playita*, pause, then retrieve a beach treasure which finds its way into a satchel tagged for Anchorage; city cousins visiting their rural counterparts dart across the beach a la Easter egg hunt style and screech with glee as tiny fingers close around a new fragment. My friend adopts a stretch of beach, cleans it up and turns it into a treasure trove for the young and young-at-heart. How cunning. I sense this old boy might have been a teacher in a former life.

This entry posts on Earth Day, I urge all to watch for those who make seemingly minute differences. They are out there, aren't we?

Off to Corrales   (May)

For Diana and me it is just another day in paradise, but for our new friends from San Diego, it is an entry into their Yelapa record book. The proprietor of Okley Activities and Excursions, ferries us to Corrales for the day aboard his new boat. Geographically, Corrales occupies the southern entry point into Banderas Bay. It is a beautiful crescent beach with seemingly only one structure, a primitive restaurant off to one side. Well, this "primitive restaurant" crafts 5+ star meals, much of which exit the sea that morning or while you are eating. Allow me to illustrate:

Courses:
#1 Caracol (sea snail) Ceviche
#2 Thinly sliced scallops chilled and marinated in lime juice
#3 Freshly steamed wild rice with jalapenos/carrots
#4 Pan seared octopus, olive oil and garlic
#5 Grilled lobster garnished in butter and garlic
#6 Grilled red snapper also in butter and garlic

All paired with the coldest beer in Cabo Corrientes

We are busy snapping pictures as the courses arrive; by the time the red snapper lands on our table, we loose all self-control and cast cameras aside. There is no menu and the presentations vary based upon the morning harvest from the sea. This is a must do trip.

The Departure

I return to Yelapa after dropping off my best friend, my wife, Diana, at the airport. She begins her latest adventure *al norte*. Her energies will be apportioned between her sister in Los Angeles, her parents and younger sister in Palm Desert and her two adult children (one of whom is expecting our first grandchild in mid-August) in San Diego.

There will be countless hours spent cajoling her adult siblings into whatever projects they avoid, evenings of dueling televisions on full tilt from opposite ends of her parent's home. And the request by her daughter that mom be her birth coach. Life will be busy.

Nikki, our English Shepherd, and I remain in Yelapa until early August. The summer heat/humidity become oppressive; we are seasoned veterans and will survive (define survival). Those of you who spend time away from a spouse or even recently experienced a departure understand well the intensity of the early hours of being solo. I clomp up stairs to *Casa Azul*; a pair of small sandals awaits. A paper-thin pink petal from a nearby flowering tree resides on our mat. I flash upon the frailty I feel in my relationship and as a human in general. Did I express the most sincere of tones in my last "I love you?" Might that parting hug have lingered just a tad longer?

Nikki is delighted to see me; yet her eyes quickly communicate that the number returning is less than the number departing. I explain to her that it is complicated. She and I journey through the next few months knowing that we are two thirds complete. *Que le vaya bien querida, que le vaya bien* (May you travel well, my love).

When a partner is absent, even temporarily, we alter our lives minutely. The bath towels last twice as long as I alternate between the two. Dishes are washed every other day but not until their accumulated presence on the counter infers that two are in residence (i.e. two wine glasses, two dinner plates,) I play music that my spouse enjoys less than I. An additional glass of wine is consumed. Nikki remains a little closer, a little longer. The bathroom door no longer requires closing. Prior to Diana's departure, I tell her warmly that I will miss her five times each day: 1) a hug in the morning; 2) breakfast 3) lunch 4) dinner 5) a hug at night. She seems less than moved. Perhaps it is the fact that 60% of the times that I miss her relate to meal creation. The kid is sharp! That's one of many reasons I love her.

Manual Labor (Part I)

We have all walked past construction sites and marveled at the technology of the event? It is invariably some ground-based or roof-mounted crane that attracts our focus. This machine forms the nerve center, spine, and musculature of the project. Without it, the structure would remain countless lines criss-crossing a sheet of paper on a drafting table.

Home/construction loans do not exist in

Yelapa. Construction is funded out of savings. An owner builds/improves/expands a project as cash is available. When the funds are exhausted, the project pauses. It must sound primitive to those north of the border. There are no high-rises here. Our tallest structures peak at four levels and are cantilevered into the hillside. All are assembled block by block utilizing nerve centers, spines and musculatures of human cranes. It is mesmerizing to watch.

A young couple lives across the street. Two weeks back, materials pile up in the open area adjacent to their home: rebar, gravel, cement and solid concrete blocks. The project, the building of a second story living space, began roughly ten days ago. In that time, virtually all the materials are deployed. Ok, I hear you saying, no big deal. Allow me to further explain that this project involves a total of two workers. One, is the senior craftsman who handles every aspect once the materials are delivered onto the roof. The second individual is the Materials Transportation Specialist. I watch this man stack three concrete blocks onto a platform, then shift the load to the crotch created in his shoulder by extending his arm to the top of the blocks. He walks across the yard, climbs a primitive ladder (no hand rails) to the roof and delivers the blocks to some pre-determined spot. He repeats the process again and again and again. He is clad in standard Yelapa attire: t-shirt, shorts and flip-flops. He wears no steel-toe high-top work boots, no yellow hard hat, no gloves nor kidney-belt. There is no forklift; there is one person, a human crane. He performs this task for seven hours per day. The following morning, he returns: lifting, carrying, climbing, depositing, repeat.

The thought of his just compensation never enters my mind. That is a matter between him and the owner; not my business. What I do think about is the physical fatigue, the pain and agony that would rack every molecule of my being from my toenails to the hair follicles atop my head. Over the past ten days I have grown to respect this individual immensely. When the project pauses, I will miss the humility his presence evokes.

I've been Adopted

Volumes exist detailing the connection between stress and mental/physical health. When we experience stress, our brain, via some synaptic Situation Room, begins preparing for war. The more prolonged the stress, the more extensive the preparations. Once the plans are formulated, war is declared—on yourself!!! Headaches, intestinal discomfort, sleep issues all invite some type/s of substance/s abuse. The picture deteriorates rapidly.

Flying flat into the face of logic (a practice not unknown to me), I head to my office when I am stressed. For those of you unfamiliar with my "office," allow me to create an image. Picture a raised platform roughly 5' X 10'. Half of the space is occupied by a rack supporting six kayaks. The other half is open. Here, I position my lounge chair. The chair and I shift to retain the cover afforded a gigantic fig tree. All senses are drawn to the sea that lies a handful of meters to the front.

During one such therapeutic session, I become aware of two young girls. Their hands are stuffed with a variety of treasures in preparation for some adventure. Unaware of my presence, they climb into a beached *panga*, intricately arrange their treasures across one of the benches and commence to play out some imaginary scene replete with action and dialogue. A smile creeps across my lips. One girl spots me. Instead of recoiling in embarrassment, the pair collects their props and relocates to my platform. They are no more concerned with my presence than the frigate birds carving celestial figure eights above me.

Suddenly, they dash to the sea. They frolic and squeal as kids are meant to do. They return, shell fragments in tow and extend their little brown hands in my direction. The younger one states that these are treasures from the sea and that they will provide memories of my visit to Yelapa. I am warmed by their thoughtfulness, and alert them that I live here. They process the information briefly then return to the imaginary drama that earlier occupied them. Time passes, my new friends gather their treasures leaving the shells for me. We bid each other *"adios."* The smile they shared lingers.

Since then, the three of us reconvene frequently. There is always a cheery *"hola"* which begins our encounter and the parting *"adios"* which concludes it. In between are countless words that communicate experiences since our last meeting. I understand perhaps one fourth of what they say; it is my listening that pleases them, not my response. The shell fragments remain atop my platform. They serve as permanent props awaiting a future episode of "imagining." My smile resides there also, among the shells.

Theory of Evolution

Yelapa is in the jungle; not adjacent to, not nearby, and certainly not just a short distance from but in the jungle. The ocean that occupies our little bay is merely an extension. Those who came of age during the original Tarzan series recall warrior pygmies, rivers teaming with crocodiles and the ever-popular pet chimpanzee, Cheetah. Yelapa contains none of these. What it does contain is an ever changing variety of migratory birds displaying gorgeous plumage; an endless raft of flying-crawling-climbing insects whose body structures frequently replicate miniature dinosaurs; an anthology of dragonflies, moths and butterflies speckled with vibrant colors in unimaginable designs. And amidst all this marvel, reside a pair of bushy-tailed squirrels. They seem out of place but appear to be much at home. Alas, the jungle is welcoming.

Living in the midst of this vibrancy, I frequently wax philosophical. During one such "waxing," I stumbled upon a thought that demanded further consideration. If man/woman, who now revels in his/her ability to control the entirety of the environment, was meant to occupy this pinnacle of domination, then why wasn't he/she the first to occupy the planet? Then all subsequent entrants could occupy their assigned places early on. But that's not what happened. We were the last to join the group, why? I have a theory.

What if at the end of the week, millennium or whenever, the animals convened and decided that all-in-all life was pretty good but that they would enjoy some intermittent comic relief. A cross-species commission is formed; the concept of "man" emerges. Think about it, most of man's time is occupied by misguided attempts to imitate other animals' behaviors.

Allow me to illustrate:

Shelter-Animals create efficient, protective structures out of nearby materials. Man shaves off the top of a hill, hauls in timber from a thousand miles away, utilizes multi-ton machinery to construct a two-story, 3500 square foot home for a family of three.

Employment-Animals collectively engage in work that benefits the community. Man's work has absolutely no bearing on the overall needs of the community but is designed to satiate his desire to acquire more "stuff" for the shelter just mentioned.

Recreation-Animals infuse play and frivolity into most of what they do whether it's creating family housing or trying to tidy up the common area. Man remains consumed by the obsession with "stuff" and therefore has no time to play. What few exceptions exist relate to Monday's which are play-days legislated by powerful lobbyists representing the greeting card and chocolate industries.

Life-Animals realize that birth and death are everyday cycles. Man invents multi-billion dollar industries crafted around these naturally recurring activities.

Alas, we are an entertaining lot. Does anyone else hear that hyena off in the distance?

Marina Day   (June)

Absolute silence defines the morning following a major *fiesta* in our village. The canine corp delays its piercing yaps while the roosters vanish to some poultry retreat. Family elders engaged in street sweep-and-greet delay. The air is stilled by a fog that suspends any observable animation. Heads full of brew from the prior night have yet to awaken and throb. It is the quiet before the hangover storm.

The first weekend of June is designated *Día de la Marina* to celebrate the activities of all those who live, work and play on the sea. The celebration begins mid-day Saturday with families in *pangas* floating a wreath in Banderas Bay to honor those who have gone before. When the boats return, the party begins. There is the opening egging as children, big and small, chase others to anoint the pursued with the fruit of the hen. A DJ presses the power button and techno music

(???) blares from four speakers, each the size of a port-a-potty. Locals offer ceviche and finger food. An actual *panga* pulled up onto the beach, courtesy of *El Buly*, functions as a cooler and grants temporary refuge to countless cases of *Corona* and *Pacifico*. Swim suit clad young women undulate to primordial drum beats. Larger groups of imbibing men stare at the dancers and then find solace in patting, rubbing or scratching their overhanging bellies. Let the *fiesta* begin.

The afternoon highlight is the team climbing of a greased pole. This involves the same males mentioned above attempting to organize and then execute a plan to scale the greased pole and retrieve cash affixed to the top. By this time, the aforementioned men are neither capable of organizing nor executing anything. They tumble frequently and revel in their inabilities.

The evening is punctuated with a rodeo, Yelapa style, at the far end of the village. Additional quantities of food and beverage sustain whatever feelings of invincibility were instilled earlier. Actual *vaqueros* (cowboys), straddle immense bulls and attempt to remain affixed for several seconds. More often than not the rider is ejected; but once in a rare while one is successful and cheers erupt.

It is Sunday morning. Slight signs of life emerge. The beach party resumes at mid-day. More solid/liquid refreshments consumed, more music and undulation stared upon and more overhanging bellies in need of much patting, rubbing and scratching.

Monday arrives, as it always has. Over the next few days any evidence of this annual *fiesta* is erased. Once again the dogs bark, the roosters crow and a less frenetic level of activity revisits our village. Aaaah, *la vida tranquila* (the calm life).

Manual labor Part 2

I previously addressed the efforts of one young laborer, as he transported concrete blocks from a ground level staging area up a primitive ladder and onto a roof top. This task he performed alone and in silence seven hours a day for six straight days.

Over the intervening days, water and electrical lines are chiseled (Mexican style) into their locations. A team of two or three men are present each day hand-mixing small amounts of concrete, smoothing or grinding. Their work commences 8 ish and continues until 3 ish. This rhythm repeats six or seven times.

The most celebrated day of any

construction project is not the day it commences, nor is it the day the family moves in. (It is common in Yelapa for the family to live in the structure as it is being built. Such formalities as Certificates of Occupancy do not exist.) Back to my story— the most significant day/event in the entire construction process is the day the roof is poured. At that time, the available labor pool is marshaled to transport concrete from Point A to Point B. Today, a dozen such chaps appear with five gallon plastic buckets in tow.

A mixer is strategically placed between stacks of cement bags, gravel bags and a mountain of sand. The most senior position, aside from the foreman atop the structure, appears to be the person in possession of a large flat-edged shovel. That individual dictates to the four-member Mixing Crew the amount of an ingredient required to craft the best batch of concrete. There is no discussion. The remaining gang of eight performs the heavy lifting, literally. They cue up next to the mixer, receive a quantity of grey sludge, hoist it onto a shoulder, hike up to the roof to await the foreman's direction as to the appropriate dump site. This process continues uninterrupted for more than five hours. No one, I repeat, no one stops to talk, smoke, drink, pat, rub or scratch anything the entire time. Apparently the following construction mantra prevails "Concrete waits for no man."

As the final pail is poured, hoisted, transported and dumped, the group of twelve amasses under the shade. A few light cigarettes, others retrieve bottles of water; the majority slump forward with forearms resting on knees. They disband as uneventfully as they amassed. Some ponder a shower and a siesta, others a cold beer while some relish their fist full of pesos to save towards their own construction project----- someday.

Bears in the Jungle

You know that bears do not inhabit the jungle, right? So just what is it that I am attempting to say? Ah, I thought you'd never ask.

In Yelapa, there are several really large men. We're talking the size of tackles for the New England Patriots. These are big guys. The first one with whom you are likely to come in contact is Sipriano. Along with an ever-present orange Truper wheelbarrow (*caretilla*), he plies his trade as baggage porter, cargo hauler or just general disseminator of Yelapa information. His toothy smile beams from one end of the town pier to the other. He and I share abusive greetings, he shouts "hey *gordo*" (fat man) and I respond "hey *flaco*" (skinny man). We chuckle. For a fee, Sipriano will transport your luggage or packages to their destination. He traverses the hills of town many times each day. His body is bisected by a black kidney belt. Instead of granting him a svelte hour-glass appearance, it looks more like a black rubber band stretched tautly around the center of a giant potato. If it is intended to add to his comedic ambiance, then it accomplishes this well. He is a gentle giant and a trusted villager.

Our second bear, known to anyone who has visited Yelapa, is Pahuelas. He can be spotted at a great distance, or even out in the bay, as the result of his signature piece of apparel—a Rasta hat. He is a member of the family who owns/operates *Tacos y Mas* and the Rosewood Shop on the path up to the town falls. He also free lances as an outboard motor mechanic. His travels invariably include a handful of disciples. A pony tail descends his back; an infectious laughter accompanies this man like a ray of sunshine. When he chuckles, which is more often than not, his entire girth engages. He is a friend to all.

Our third bear is Sammy. Ah, where does one begin when describing Sammy? This gentleman is "somewhat" challenged in height yet abundantly gifted in girth; something akin to a ripe grapefruit with little legs. This physical set-up does not bode itself to walking the streets of Yelapa, so he relies heavily on a blue *moto* (ATV). Now *motos* make noise, the older the *moto*, the more noise. Sammy has a really old *moto*, yet he is the only human in town who can be heard a block down the road while revving his *moto* up a hill. He possesses a voice capable of disintegrating wine bottles two kilometers away. Sammy's occupational specialty is doing things that no one else wants to do: 1) he picks up and collects anything which is metal (refrigerators, washing machines, sinks etc.) transports them in his *panga* and sells the metal for scrap. As a result of his efforts, perhaps a dozen *panga* loads of rusty, unsightly metal are removed. 2) he is available on short notice to haul people and stuff to Boca as well as pick up people and stuff from Boca—naturally there is a fee. 3) of late, there is a sign on Sammy's front door— Organic Chicken and Duck Eggs for sale. No telling what could be next, but you can bet he'll be on it. If you ever need him, he's easy to find. Walk to his house next to Yuri's Market; look inside; if you see Sammy sitting on his *moto* in his living room watching TV, then he's available.

These are but three of the bears that inhabit Yelapa. Feel free to feed or offer drink to them. They don't bite. Much to the contrary, they typify the warmth of our village.

The Rain

Yelapa is taunted the prior two nights with the beginning of the rainy season. Each evening delivers sprinkles, a minor light show and cool morning temps. For a village which hasn't seen moisture since last September, this is an event. Last night, the real thing lands. Intermittently, for nearly four hours, we experience rain, lightening, thunder and a light show surpassing any 4th of July celebration. Villagers knew *"la lluvia"* has returned.

Like any event in a small community, it demands discussion. During *birria* at Ray's, the topic absorbs every word of every moment. Invariably, the discourse drifts to where were you when the "big one" hit? Allow me to respond. The storm moves in roughly 9:15pm ish. Nikki and I are considering a movie. In the Bay of Banderas, the arrival of a storm is predictable. From the moment you observe the first lightening (*relampago*) and its associated thunder (*trueno*), there is a ten minute interval until the rain begins. This is rumored to relate to an ancient pact between nature and the indigenous peoples of *Cabo Corrientes* so that they could safely return their *pangas* to shore. No one seems certain.

This storm follows the prescribed ritual. By 9:30 pm it is in full tilt. Lightening, thunder and rain merge, disaggregate and merge again for the ensuing four hours. Now that's a typical Yelapa rain storm. I have never experienced lightening and its sibling, thunder as we have it here. The flashes continue to outline a portion of the horizon for a half minute of so. Brother thunder enters the arena seamlessly and crescendos to a point of nuclear detonation. At each of these intersections an enormous deluge of moisture occurs.

This is not an event which endears itself to canines. Nikki, our English Shepherd, seeks shelter at the first flash, forget waiting for the thunder. However, last night was slightly different. We both retire early. As the storm plays out across the sky; Nikki and I settle. Fifteen, maybe twenty minutes pass and BAM, a bolt nails a spot of turf to the front of our *casita*. While I levitate a foot, Nikki, already sheltering under the bed, burrows through the terra cotta tile.

Upon departing *Casa Azul* this morning, I notice the array of greens adorning the trees and brush along the path. The rains dissolve any hint of dirt resident for months. The rocks in the path, which travel guides reference as romantic cobble stones, shine as if individually buffed.

I greet my friends at Ray's. We share the ritual of *birria* together. The calm of the bay, the morning sounds of the jungle and a humming bird flitting effortlessly all remind me of why I live here. The mounting humidity reminds me that I depart for a few months.

The Rain-The back story

Since the rains returned, there's a palpable release of tension. The uncertainty which accompanies the month of June relates to the timing of that return. Once June begins, the village has been without rain since September, eight months. Average humidity begins at 40%, skin and eyes remain moist, and feminine hair explodes into frizz. There's a reason why they refer to this belt on the globe as The Tropics.

Walk back with me to the first week in June. The village is upbeat as the certain arrival of inches of moisture will brighten the greens of the jungle even further. The lagoon, fed by the Tuito River, warehouses frog laden pools which shrink daily. Week two arrives with a history that our weather lives will soon be altered. Week three follows and concern stalks our pathways. Afternoon clouds roll in and embrace the mountain ridges but not a drop is dripped. Worry lines reside across the foreheads of the elders. Conversation is monopolized by this single topic. Week four begins: day one-nothing; day two-a twenty minute sprinkle; day three-a two hour moderate rain complete with the requisite lightening/thunder dynamics; day four—all hell breaks loose with twin two-hour bursts. The associated lightening/thunder creates a world class display.

Creeks surge to join the Tuito; the river angrily attacks its banks. During the night, this anger drives the flow over a twelve foot tall sandbar which lay undisturbed for the past eight months. Silt is re-deposited by early morning turning our entire bay a creamy coffee brown. Another testimony to the furor of Mother Nature. In a pair of days it clears.

Audible sighs ascend like dialogue bubbles above the rooftops. We shift into Plan-R (rain). *Pangas* without bilge pumps must be hand-bailed succeeding each deluge, whether day or night. One or two will sink while tethered to their moorings; they always do. Socializing, shopping and dining revolve around afternoon/evening downpours whose randomness guarantees the opportunity for total personal wetness. Wash will hang on makeshift lines, and hang, and hang, and hang.

A sense of contentment returns. Village life embraces seasonal certainties: humidity, heat, power outages, tempestuous seas, water running everywhere and soon to arrive, everyone's favorite (NOT) multiple crab migrations. (A future blog posting will address this event.) While these components won't define the perfect get-a-way for much of the traveling public, they will define life in Yelapa for the next three months. The village draws comfort from these norms.

Fortune (July)

Nearly two years ago, my wife, Diana, and I are enjoying dinner out. The owner, supervises four waiters who provide excellent service. One clearly stands above the rest. He doesn't depart with your order, he speeds; he doesn't leisurely ascend and descend the four steps leading away from the dining patio, he appears to vault in both directions. He discusses in detail our dining options, the ingredients and method of preparation. We return to his station frequently. When the site closes unexpectedly in mid-March, Ray Vazquez walks a hundred meters down the main path, leases a vacant space and is up and running in less than two weeks. The rest is culinary history.

In the months which follow, we consume countless margaritas and indescribable delicacies; even more importantly, we earn the friendship of the family (Ray, Violeta,

Alexa). We now identify the furrowed brow which proclaims that the moment is not right to joke with Ray, we share the pain of Violeta's extended undiagnosed intestinal disorder that debilitates her without notice, and lastly we fall in love with the innocence of a young girl, Alexa, whose eyes glow with pride and admiration for her parents. Into this inner circle we now enter.

In a demonstration of their trust, the family offers and I accept the role of *padrino* (godparent) for the occasion of Alexa's sixth grade graduation. This requires that I stand with her during the ceremony. Unbeknown to me, this also involves accepting the invitation to be Alexa's partner for the first waltz following her graduation. Clearly, this declares her newly gained maturity. Now there is something fanciful about a Straus waltz yet here is one being played, via DJ, in a small rural village in Mexico and I am dancing with a special young lady. We dip, twirl and at just the right moment came to rest. The experience is capped with a hug; a memory for the balance of my years.

Nearly a week passes. Villagers stop me and comment on my new status. Tonight, the family and I will enjoy dinner together; Diana will be spoken of and missed. For a man (me) whose circle of friends tends to look more like a triangle, this is a big deal. There are a other stories here in Yelapa where "outsiders" have become insiders through the mutual trust that evolves between them and a local family. I count Diana and me, among those fortunate few (*los afortunados*).

Country Cousin/City Cousin

Yelapa opens its piers, beaches and *palapa* doors to visitors year round. The surge occurs November thru April; the weather is perfect, the skies are clear and total tropical immersion is just a margarita away. As summer takes root in May, the surge diminishes to a trickle and locals settle in for what they ironically call "the dry" season. The May/June time frame offers a dramatic reminder that the tourist-based economy, like the environment, is fragile. All but a handful of restaurants batten their hatches and the village adopts survival mode.

July ushers in the end of the academic year. Graduations require planning. Countless family parties demand organizing and scheduling. The last activity, scheduling, is the more rigorous as it is unforgivable to schedule your event at the same moment as another. No doubt, somewhere on a living room wall in Yelapa is a PERT diagram that tracks all such happenings. By mid-July, the party pandemonium ceases. Parents and god-parents sigh relief.

Mexican family vacations are determined by their children's holidays from school. For the next six weeks, the bulk of our visitors will be Mexican families. Their stay involves but a few days or a weekend and back they trek. They populate the main beach, drink beer from transported coolers and spend relatively little money. A trickle continues from north of the border, or even the border beyond, but they are few.

There is yet another genre of visitor who ventures to Yelapa. Each of the four founding family elders is born into a family of nine to eleven siblings. That generation replicates the family size into which they grew. The following generation tends to downsize by roughly fifty percent but remains sizable. You begin to sense the feeling of community existent in our village; virtually everyone is related to everyone else.

As family members depart Yelapa for the allure of the big city, they continue to procreate. Those family members, along with their broods, return throughout the summer. The children are easy to spot as they wear bright new shirts, shorts, and shoes. I call them "the city cousins." They speak rapidly, and appear uncomfortable at the lack of street lights or designated crossing zones. There is a discernible absence of their previously hovering parents. Approaching *motos* startle them and cause them to scatter. Their hosts, the local kin, "country cousins" are initially entertained by these antics but over time share the requisite survival skills.

Hornos and barbeques dormant for months reactivate. All manner of cooking aromas arise. It is a time for celebrating the family. By the following Monday or sometime mid-week, the visiting parents all manage to slip away unceremoniously. You see where this heads, right? Their progeny stay for another two weeks or so.

I live at ground zero for the largest family clan in Yelapa. As I write, there are at least five "city cousins" engaged with a like number of "country cousins." The game of choice appears to be chase. They chase the chickens in the yard across the path. They chase the garobos which venture out of the numerous rock piles. They chase a pair of squirrels which dart overhead from branch to branch. When nothing else moves, and generally as a last resort, they chase each other. All the while squealing with joy, inclusive of barking dogs, nervous chickens cackling and roosters crowing. It is a cacophony which repeats itself in a hundred village households each day. It assaults my definition of tranquility. Alas, I remain, on occasion, a stranger in what is, on occasion, a strange land.

The Sun and I

Visitors trek to Mexico to enjoy beautiful beaches, warm water, fabulous food and cold beverages. An unfortunate percentage of them ruin their vacations based upon actions taken within the first hours. Allow me to illustrate: John/Mary Smith arrive in PV (Puerto Vallarta) late morning. They depart winter's gloom to enjoy all that Vallarta offers. Following a shuttle to some beach-front hotel, they check in; dash to the room, leap into swimwear and sprint for the pool. The afternoon is punctuated with intermittent swim-ups to the pool bar. Circa 5 p.m. they re-enter the lobby and become mindful that the air conditioned environment fails to comfort them. Dark glasses are removed; the couple stares at each other in horror. You have observed this scenario, right? Perhaps even participated in it? The next few days will present challenges for this duo. Sunburn is dangerous and can prove fatal.

SPF (sun protective factor) and UVA/UVB (ultra violet A/B rays) are forces to be reckoned with here in the tropics.

Recommendations (prior to departure):

1. Acquire sunglasses which afford 99-

100% UVA/UVB protection.
2. Purchase sunscreen (the term sunblock is not allowed in the USA) with an SPF 30+. The container should include the phrase "Broad Spectrum." This means that protection is afforded against both types of ultra-violet rays.

Use these guidelines when applying:

1. Apply initial coating 30 minute before exposure.
2. Re-apply 30 minutes after initial exposure.
3. Re-apply after swimming, sweating or wiping
4. Re-apply every two hours that you are exposed

The UV rating changes throughout the day. If you arrive at the beach mid-morning, the UV rating is likely to be 4 (Moderate Risk). At mid-day, that reading approaches 11 (Extreme Risk); levels of 13 are not uncommon. Avoid the agony of being ill prepared.

Travels with Nikki

When humans travel internationally, we investigate health hazards, documentation requirements, security precautions, currency exchange rates, climate variances and dietary differences; and all that just for an extended weekend. If our travels include the family pet, the planning becomes more complex.

When Diana and I relocate to Yelapa, our plans include transporting our three year old English Shepherd, Nikki. I research the requirements. Our carrier, Alaska Airlines, offers extensive information regarding the importation of domestic animals into Mexico. The checklist is complete and concise. I follow the list with exactitude. It requires the following: the procuring of an approved travel crate, current vaccinations, evidence of annual rabies shot, a veterinarian's signed health statement in English and Spanish, an international certificate, and a copy of the practitioner's actual state license. The airlines requires confirmed passage twenty-four hours before departure and a fee. Alaska Airlines alerts us that Nikki will be traveling in a pressurized, climate controlled environment. We deposit her two hours prior to departure and reclaim her in Puerto Vallarta within thirty minutes of arrival.

Shortly, Nikki and I will return to San Diego to link up with Diana, and assist in welcoming the first grandchild (a girl). I begin my research into required documentation. An online visit to Alaska Airlines now identifies a link to the CDC regarding importation of animals into the USA. After plowing through countless pages on their site, I locate a reference to individual state's Veterinary Services Department. Next stop, California VSD; the only documentation reference is the requirement for a rabies vaccination within the prior twelve months. An email sent to confirm this single issue results in a response which refers me to the CDC website. Arg!

Yesterday morning, Nikki and I are off on an early *panga* to PV, a walk down the *Malecon*, a taxi to Pitillal to the veterinarian-- two shots, a return taxi to Los Muertos Pier and a return *panga* to Yelapa. We open the door to *Casa Azul* at 12:21 pm, roughly five hours after our departure. Health Certificate in hand evidencing current rabies vaccination; we are good to go.

Traveling is stressful; with a pet--doubly so. Allow plenty of time to do your homework regarding the requirements both outbound and inbound. If you are going for a brief stay, consider leaving fido/fluffy at home with a sitter or in a kennel. Maybe they would like a break too.

Mr. Fix-It (August)

I have owned several homes over the past four decades. As a result, I acquire the "fix-it" skills of replacing a washer in a dripping faucet, removing and clearing a sink trap, installing a new electrical plug (including a GFCI) and caulking around door molding. Despite numerous editions of How to Do Anything: A-Z as presents from my spouse; I neither display the ability nor the desire to improve in this regard. This does not bode well in my domestic environment.

Fast forward to our Yelapa relocation two years ago. We rent and improve a brand new, never occupied two bedroom, one bath *casita*. A local builder assists in locating the property and supervises the completion. Five months later, we arrive to embrace the tranquility of paradise.

While cosmetically our place could be featured in *Casita Digest*, certain areas demand attention. The landlord, who lives directly below us, fails to connect the sewer until two days prior to our arrival. Therefore, our builder does not have the opportunity to check the charged system. We experience hot water in the toilet, and the reversal of every hot/cold fixture in the dwelling. In passing, hot water in the commode is not an entirely unpleasant sensation. However, once we consider the repetitive impact with our on-demand water heater, the possibility of cracking a cold porcelain bowl whilst sitting astride it and the early disintegration of the wax donut seal, our concern grows. Three plumbers and thirty days later, the issue is resolved.

We instruct the builder to install thresholds and sweeps on each door. This is not SOP for Mexican construction. He is so proud that the items are in place that as we arrive he points them out. Two nights later we sit motionless as a six inch scorpion scales a living room wall. A few days following that incident, we notice a growing presence of mega-wasps. A room-to-room search reveals small mud nests affixed to the two steel I-beams supporting the roof. These inch and a half hatchlings awaited our arrival before introducing themselves. Swatters within constant reach, we spend fourteen days swinging and ducking. Wasps are aggressive.

As I pass through life's portals Into the autumn of my existence, I exude tolerance and acceptance. Diana, on the other hand, remains in the summer of her vitality, and exhibits no evidence of either. You can see where this is headed, right? Once again, I am responsible for another unilateral decision which exhausts our fiscal resources, relocates our little band to some remote patch of a foreign country, and now we, like Dante, are staring at each other wondering how many levels of hell we have yet to experience. The tranquil life remains illusive.

In Mexico, tequila is the elixir of life. Its clarity and blend-ability allow it to be infused secretly into other liquids. These include, but are not limited to: bottled water, coffee, juices of all sorts, soy milk and smoothies. Tranquility has returned to our *casita*. We peer out our bay window for hours. We share our hopes, dreams and await our future together. Even Nikki appears more sedate. I am forever indebted to the Jose Cuervo Corporation.

The Countdown

Friday afternoon, Nikki and I will board a sky ship to launch towards San Diego. I cannot help but conjure up the images associated with a certain Woody Allen movie as technicians are seated at a master console overseeing all brain functions. As I recall they were also planning a launch.

If you are a visitor to my blog, you know about my favorite restaurant, Ray's Place, operated by my favorite people: Ray, Violeta and Alexa. It is no surprise that the finest food in Yelapa is produced by the finest people. I am fortunate to be considered a part of their family. As an aside, they will open in October at their new location. My best wishes and future patronage will travel with them.

Today is Sunday, right? And what happens on Sunday, class? The children look up adoringly and respond in angelic tones, "*birria.*" Well done, class! Today, I consumed my last Sunday *birria* for perhaps the next two months. Good byes are exchanged. A twinge of sadness clouds my return to *Casa Azul.*

Our village remains quiet over the next two months. Schools throughout Mexico begin Monday. The last *panga* full of visiting Mexican nationals will depart for Puerto Vallarta this afternoon. Tomorrow morning will invite the ritual of the early rising of the teacher and his wife, who live below me (they have yet to figure out how to move chairs quietly); the gaiety of conversations returns between the passing elementary students; and the parents of pre-schoolers parked down the path. New shoes and uniforms are worn. All backpacks carry the hopes and aspirations of parents, grandparents and fellow villagers. It is an event of renewal.

I have yet to experience the month of September in Yelapa. Locals assure me that as the heavy rains arrive, so also arrive the heavy tuna. Every fishing boat, *panga*, boogie board or stray piece of floating tree trunk will have a kid in it or on it launching a hand line. Refrigerators and freezers are filled. Any excess is sold in Puerto Vallarta. This sea bounty presents the only money-making opportunity until tourism returns in mid-November. Life in paradise is difficult.

My countdown continues. My last *pozole* tomorrow night, my last trip to the market, my last bag of trash, my last margarita and dinner with Ray and the family. Friday morning my last fruit smoothie (pineapple, papaya, mango, granola, honey, yogurt). In English when someone departs we say "good bye." It's clipped and final. In Spanish, we choose from *"andale pues," "hasta luego," "que le vaya bien,"* all of which are open-ended. These phrases grant both the well-wisher and the well-wished the expectation that they will meet again. As Nikki and I trek through Yelapa, I will hear and respond to all of these, resolute that in a few months, we will meet again.

The Remains (September)

Dianne and I cycle through family. Moments with our new granddaughter, are indeed special as we flash back to the infant her mother was some three plus decades earlier. Now, we hop a plane and head eastward to visit my brother and his wife.

Whilst awaiting our departure from San Diego, I become aware of a mature sailor in spotless white dress regalia circling the waiting area. He vanishes; then returns repeating this sequence several times. The sides of his shaved head glistened while his crew cut appears capable of deflecting asteroids. The row upon row of ribbons on his chest defines a career serviceman of vast experience. He is an impressive chap. He vanishes again.

Thirty minutes prior to our East Coast arrival, the captain makes the following announcement, "We have a military escort on board this afternoon. He is accompanying the remains of a fallen service member." This disclosure explains the presence of the sailor. The captain's disclosure invites a moment of silent respect punctuated with subdued applause. His choice of words lingers: "the remains." It sounds as if the service member is less than whole. This nomenclature disturbs me. I have known armed conflict. I experienced dead soldiers both friendly and foe, but never thought of them as "remains." It sounds impersonal; something akin to military jargon like "collateral damage" (dead people, destroyed buildings) or "unavoidable civilian casualties" (the killing of innocent men, women, children). What would be missing from those families would not be the "remains" of someone, it would be that person in their entirety.

Our aircraft taxis to the gate. The captain asks that we remain seated until the escort exits to resume his duties. Quiet applause accompanies his departure. We deplane.

CHAPTER 2
THE THIRD YEAR

I'm Back!!! (November)

Summer is a busy time. First, a trip to San Diego by Diana, the expectant grandmother, who helps prepare the nest. Baby arrives; two weeks later I'm on scene. Out to Palm Desert to see family; back to San Diego. Assist the new mom then off to Asheville, North Carolina for a stint with my brother and his wife. Back to San Diego to recharge with a baby "fix." Next we fly to Chicago to enjoy a visit with Yelapa friends Erin and Patrick. Back to San Diego, out to Palm Desert to pick up Nikki, return to San Diego. Fly to Puerto Vallarta, snag a van at the airport, board the water taxi to Yelapa. Last leg: hail Sipriano at the town pier to assist with our bags, say *"hola"* to half the village (give hugs to the other half) and collapse on the couch. You're not buying this I can tell. Over the summer the blog crosses two milestones: 1) one year anniversary; 2) records 4000 visits.

One travel anecdote demands retelling. We board our flight in San Diego with one dog crate, one large tote, two backpacks and one laptop case. We exit the plane in Puerto Vallarta with two backpacks, proceed through Mexican Customs, and walk half-way down a football length corridor before realizing that—yep, you guess it—I do not have my laptop case. I sprint to the Immigration Area. You cannot retrace your steps through immigration. I hail a woman in the office and recount my tale. Over the next few moments, she attempts to reach Alaska Airlines via telephone. Realizing my desperation and the realities of a departure of the same aircraft, she grabs a maintenance worker with a radio and asks that he contact the airlines; no luck. Immigration Officers, like Customs Officials, are not known for their customer service skills. I found an exception, perhaps my former assessment was harsh.

There are airline personnel in the baggage claim area, right? Diana journeys ahead to retrieve our luggage plus Nikki. By the time I arrive, she has engaged an individual and communicates our plight. Following all kinds of radio chatter and several brief absences, the representative alerts us that the case is located and will be at the ticket counter in the front of the airport. Problem solved, right?????? Not so fast!!! Inside the case are Nikki's documents for re-entry into Mexico. Without these, we cannot clear the Vet Check or Customs. Back to the Alaska Air Rep who states that the case can be brought downstairs but it will take "some time". We smile, thank her; we have no choice. Ten minutes later, she returns sporting a large toothy grin and our case. Nikki clears inspection. We receive the coveted green light from the Customs Agent and off we head, free at last.

The closing moments of our Yelapa return flirt with disaster. But for two wonderful women who empathize with our plight, we would have been doomed. No doubt, we will never see either of them again. IF any of you experience some type of travel snafu, there are angels out there. Treat them well.

P.S. Did I say how fabulous it is to be home in Yelapa with my wife and Nikki?

Renewal

Word association--"renewal?" Magazine subscription, pharmacy prescription, auto registration??? Ask a Yelapan the same question; they will tell you about the jungle following the summer rains; the returning sea animals as first the manta ray, then the humpbacks and ultimately the tuna renew the Bay of Banderas. Lastly, they identify their physical renewal as temperatures and humidity recede from the nineties bracket and settle comfortably into the seventies.

November ushers in the high-season. Restaurants fine-tune their menus, lodge keepers apply fresh paint on anything that doesn't move faster than their brush, water taxi drivers raise their rates slightly to offset summer losses and I am hard at work spiffing my office and my kayaks. These are all forms of renewal.

Travel Note

Yelapa is a garden paradise populated with warm and friendly people. Eye contact and a sincere *"hola"* will introduce you. While our village is inviting to all, it must be said that there are a few who should not consider the trip. Yelapa is a village of cobblestone paths and hills. The elderly should not be placed at risk either by their use of the water taxi or by their limited endurance. If you are traveling with older parents, please prioritize their safety. Their travel experience is better served by remaining in Puerto Vallarta. Those with mobility limitations should likewise remain in PV. Enough said.

A New Season

A certain excitement arises when friends return. Such is the case on Sunday as John/Tamara and their Scotty, Chloe, land from Fairbanks, Alaska. We have already enjoyed two dinners together plus an hour's worth of kayaking. Welcome back!!!

An update on Ray's Place; they are open Tuesday thru Saturday for dinner, Sunday for *birria*, closed Monday. Hours may expand in the future to include breakfast and lunch. One of Ray's enormous beef, chicken or portobello hamburgers paired with the cold beverage of choice is a must for any mid-day traveler. Remember each entree and libation is individually crafted. It is going to take longer, but oh, so worth the wait. Last night they were packed. Tip: leave your watch and cell phone in a secure spot in your *palapa*. Grant yourself the opportunity to absorb the aroma of your selection before it reaches your table. You're on Yelapa time now.

Last evening, a light mist commences. As if to herald the new day, at mid-night we are engulfed in a moderate rain shower. This continues for twelve hours. Within that timeline, in typical Yelapan fashion, electrical power ceases. As of this writing (on battery power), there is a high cloud ceiling, the bay is calm but coffee colored from river silt. Off in the distance, a generator runs.

Wednesday evening brings the first humpback whale sighting of the season. The female spends a half hour outside our bay. The display reaches its zenith as she rolls to slap the surface with an enormous side fin. The entire village is abuzz. Ah, the simple life.

Busier Week

All restaurants are open. The foot traffic

increases daily. Peter and Ann arrive from Bellingham, WA. They are world travelers whose roots reach to the United Kingdom. Yelapa is an annual stop on their itinerary. Diana and I were delighted to offer them assistance after a vicious water spirit attacked Ann's phone, and Peter's laptop recharger adopted permanent siesta mode. The message was clear----they are not intended to depart tomorrow as originally scheduled. They will return to *Casa Azul* for wine this afternoon to check email and alert the "fam" that all is well.

Two dolphins enter our bay. These are large, adult animals that cruise for a half hour in search of just the right morsel. Additionally, a manta ray pops up next to a man on a stand-up paddle board. If the manta's face mirrored anything close to the expression of the paddler, then each was surprised to see the other. The paddle boarder remained upright while the manta flopped back into the bay.

The wedding virus is in full swing. No less than four ceremonies in the past five days. An evening soiree on the main beach last night reached its zenith with the release of a hundred aerial lanterns. I'm uncertain of their environmental impact. Perhaps, they are constructed from wild, not processed rice paper.

The last event is the Revolution Day celebration. This is a national holiday in observance of the Mexican triumph over the dictator, *Porfirio Diaz*. In the morning, kinder through sixth grade students parade patriotically across the main beach. The boys are attired in white shirts, black pants and crisscross paper *bandoleros* on their chests. The girls are adorned in multi-colored skirts (*faldas*) rhythmically swaying as they proceed. Older children complete acrobatic stunts. In the evening, middle school and high school students perform folkloric dances while a few brave girls sing interpretive (that's being polite) versions of Mexican standards. Homemade food compliments the festivities.

Yelapa Travel 101/102

Over the past year, I have mentioned various "travel tips" to allay anxiety regarding your trip to Yelapa. Short of combing through fifty postings, there is no single source for quick reference. This posting resolves that issue.

Assumptions: 1) your length of stay will be three to five days; 2) you will visit during the high season from mid-November thru mid-April; 3) average group size will be two to four people. Now if you are a family of eight staying from June to August, then stop reading and send me an email.

Packing (per person)
swimsuit
3 T-shirt/tank tops
1 pair of shorts for three days, two pairs for five days
1 pair of sandals for walking, 1 pair of flip-flops for inside only
hat, (minimum baseball cap)
UVA/UVB block sunglasses
1 can bug spray (deet based)
Sun screen 35 UVA/UVB
1 small LED flashlight with spare batteries
Assorted underwear and personal toiletries
1 pair ear plugs
1 camera (iphone, android, digital)

Credit/Debit Cards

If you wish to access your credit/debit cards while traveling in Mexico, alert the providers well in advance. Give them the dates of travel and when you plan to return. Few merchants accept plastic in Yelapa, while it is accepted everywhere in Puerto Vallarta. ATM (*cajeras*) machines are abundant in PV.

Currency

Bring Mexican pesos with you. Stateside banks can assist you. Their rates are the best. There are no banks or ATM machines in Yelapa. Some merchants will accept US dollars, typically at a rate of $1=10 pesos. That makes the math easy but you lose 20%

or more of your purchasing power. Plan ahead, if you can forecast your needs for the trip, consider having those funds in your pocket upon arrival.

Arrival: Puerto Vallarta International Airport

Your flight will likely arrive between 2:30pm and 4:30pm. If you are traveling as a family, you will fill out one Custom's Declaration. BUT each traveler must have his own Visitor's Visa. Retain the lower half of this form. Put in inside your passport! It is your ticket out of Mexico. Lose it, you will pay a fine and your departure will be delayed. Families move forward as a unit when the agent beckons. If you are not married to your travel companion, then each person needs a Custom's Declaration. You proceed separately past the Immigrations Officer. Hopefully, and this is a key point, you only have a carry-on sized tote and one additional item (laptop case, brief case, camera bag, purse). You accelerate past baggage claim into the Custom's Zone. Follow whatever instructions you are given as the physical layout changes frequently. IF you are asked to open luggage for inspection, do so courteously and silently. Speak only when asked a question. THE REST OF THE TIME, KEEP YOUR MOUTH SHUT!

Depart the Custom's area and briskly walk

down the hall. Do not establish eye contact or initiate conversation with the men in white shirts and pants. They are Time-Share Sharks. Once you clear the building, it is decision time. If you have only your carry-on luggage, make a left turn; walk to the end of the building; cross over the elevated pedestrian bridge to the awaiting taxis. You just saved 300 pesos ($25 USD) Tell the driver you wish to go to Los Muertos Pier-ask the cost BEFORE getting into the vehicle. (It should be around 150 pesos + tip).

There is a departing Yelapa Water Taxi at 4:30pm (ish) and another at 6pm (ish). If you are a group and/or have adequate luggage to weather the winter, exit the building. A cab supervisor will approach you. Tell him how many there are in your party, identify your luggage, he'll take it from there. Identify your destination—Los Muertos Pier—ask the cost. Before departing the airport, the cab will pull thru a toll booth—you will pay 300 pesos airport departure fee in a taxi, 500 pesos if you are in a van.

Arrival: Los Muertos Pier & Yelapa Water Taxi

As you exit your cab, two people will approach you. One is a little wiry man with a hand-truck. The second individual appears out of the Lagunita Hotel Office on your left. The former will take charge of your luggage, (remember to tip him before you depart) while the latter will sell you a water taxi ticket. DO NOT BUY A ROUND TRIP TICKET! That price will include a "handling fee" which you can avoid by purchasing your return in Yelapa. Once in the water taxi, sit as far toward the rear as possible and in the center. This will give you a dryer, smoother ride. The late afternoon seas can be angry. Consider ingesting a precautionary motion sickness tablet while at the airport. Average travel time to Yelapa, just under an hour. If you are part of large group or have multiple pieces of luggage, tip the water taxi helper upon arrival in Yelapa.

Arrival: Yelapa Pueblo

If you are staying at Lagunita Hotel or in up-river lodging, then you will depart at the Lagunita Pier. If you are staying anywhere else, then depart at the town pier. Check with your innkeeper ahead of time. Frequently, they will meet you. There are several gentlemen on the pier with wheelbarrows. For a fee, they will transport your luggage to its destination. They can be trusted. They can also be "reserved" to assist you when you depart.

Allow the pace of the village to embrace you. There are no subway/train/bus/or airline schedules here. Consider removing your watch, store your cell phone in a secure place and re-enter a moment in time which is uncluttered electronically. My personal mantra: when you are thirsty—drink; when you are hungry—eat; when you are tired--sleep. Accept the concept of "Yelapa Time." It has flourished for centuries.

There are more than a dozen great restaurants, numerous *taquerias*, 2.5 beaches (.5 for Isabel's Beach), a beautiful church, four local fishing charter/tour operators, two water falls, one major kayak rental operation (me—commercial plug), para-gliding, five markets, one laundry service, horse back riding, hiking, bird watching, butterfly watching, people watching, star gazing, live music and dancing. Or you can just settle back and allow rural Mexico to unfold around you.

A word about TripAdvisor; do your research regarding dining, lodging and activity purveyors. This web site is extremely powerful in Yelapa. When you have a great experience, and you will have many, be sure to post your thoughts on TripAdvisor. It will be much appreciated.

Local Culture
Yelapa is a casual, accepting place. A few basics bear mentioning. If you behave in a

reasonable manner in your home country, then please do so here. Public intoxication, drug use, loudness and profanity are unacceptable behaviors throughout the world. If you head to the beach but will be walking thru the village, wear a t-shirt. Walking with an open alcohol container is considered an insult. Shirts must be worn when entering the church; shorts are ok—no cellphones, food, or beverages. If you travel with your pet, when you depart for a local restaurant, leave FiFi/Fido at the apartment. Neither the restaurant owner nor the patrons have a desire to spend their evening with your pet. Once again, what would you do at home?

Security

This is a common sense issue worldwide. When not on your person, place documents, cash, and valuables in a secure site. Check with your innkeeper in advance to see if a safe is available in your *casita* or provided in a central location. Unless you are a professional photographer on assignment, consider bringing a less expensive water resistant camera to Yelapa. If you are carrying sophisticated electronics (e.g. laptop, camera, phone, etc.), bring desiccant packets. Moisture and electronics do not mix well. Our average humidity is 68%. An ounce of prevention----you know the rest, right?

Limitations

Yelapa is a village defined by hilly topography, cobble stone streets, sand and water. Climbing is required to venture almost anywhere. There are no ramps. Individuals with mobility issues, respiratory or circulatory conditions or whose general health/age renders them frail should NOT travel to Yelapa. Please do not place your loved ones at risk.

Full Swing

Yelapa is a site for destination weddings. Packages are available through Hotel Lagunita, while more adventurous types build the event from a far or thru a local contact.

This past week, the hotel hosted a one hundred fifty person wedding party. That lodging requirement exceeds their capability, meaning that participants are sprinkled throughout the village. Over the weekend, all the major restaurants are filled with wedding revelers. They are friendly and polite; welcomed additions to our local economy. The wedding occurs at dusk on Friday. A team of pink bridesmaids moves en masse like a surge of Pepto-Bismol. The groom, in full coat & tails punctuates his garb with bare feet. Shirtless local kids watch from behind bushes. And lastly, the centerpiece of the entire performance-----the bride traverses a path of newly cut palm fronds. This picturesque snow goddess glides forward toward the awaiting pink ooze.

After the briefest of ceremonies, a cheer arises, photo flashes pop and that is it. The group retires to the buffet area not to be heard the remainder of the evening. Now this is strange, since the Plan A wedding package includes three bursts of fireworks at midnight while Plan B expands that to five. Generally, from then on, it's a restless few hours of sleep as the festivities push on until 3 a.m. (ish). To our surprise neither bursts, booms nor partying disturbs our sleep.

Fall weather arrives. Day-time temperatures reach the mid-80s. Sleep time invites the accompaniment of a light cover and even a closed window. Remarkable!

In addition to the departure of the wedding entourage, others exit this week as well. Tamara/John and their dog, Chloe, return to their home in Fairbanks, AK. The Knowles, John and Becky, head to Kansas after enjoying Thanksgiving with their Yelapa family. Lastly, Diana departs Friday for San Diego to resume her full time duties as nanny-granny.

Nikki and I convene to map our daily routines: mine to include guitar practice, stationary biking, kayaking, kayak rentals, siesta taking, and the "occasional" dinner at Ray's Place. Nikki's day will be driven by breakfast, walk in the jungle, mid-morning nap, mid-afternoon nap, dinner, walk in the jungle, after dinner nap, and then sleeping all night. Our lives become less rich and more solitary.

Sweet Sunday (December)

Today is Sunday, right? That means *birria* at Ray's Place. Just returned and it was fabulous as always. Chatted with my buddies, Pahuelas and Nacho; received my Sunday hug from Alexa; all this while greeting those strolling the adjacent pathway.

Unlike couples from the North, Mexican men and women rarely dine out together. One might default to the thought that the men are "out" while the women are caring for the children. This is not necessarily the case, as fathers are frequently seen with one or more of their children. Groups of men are equally animated, albeit a bit more profane, than their female counterparts. The former tend to shout and laugh loudly, while the latter maintain a medium pitched drone punctuated by the occasional high-pitched exclamation.

There is a plethora of pueblo improvement projects in evidence this morning. I tally three major painting works-in- process. Two of these involve the white washing of tall block walls along the main path, while the third is a complete exterior makeover for the water purification plant. Our village is looking good.

There is one sensitive topic which I have heretofore avoided----geckos. These little lizard-like animals are harmless and beneficial in a dwelling. They tend to be nocturnal and feast on the tiny insects that share your abode. Geckos are territorial. An owner is fortunate to enjoy one of these as a welcomed occupant in each room. You may never be aware of their presence other than to discover tiny sausages on your counter in the morning. Those of us who live in close proximity to rental lodging in Yelapa are periodically awakened by shrill squeals. These are not the squeals which punctuate the ecstasy of an evening to remember. They proclaim raw terror. The harmless, diminutive gecko is typically the cause of this ear-shattering break in the existent tranquility? Please, do not catch your tiny guest as their bodies are soft and fragile. Simply allow them to depart on their own. Return your head to the pillow, close your eyes and smile in the awareness that nameless neighbors on both sides of you know exactly what just occurred.

Marital Bliss

Casa Azul sits atop three levels of a structure occupied by senior members of a main family in Yelapa. Everyone peers through their open door and marvels at the view of the bay. Our *casita* shares a similar view as seen through a wall of windows on the bay side.

In Yelapa, residents are responsible for tending the path in front of their dwelling. Each morning parents, grandparents and even children on the weekend, sweep the cobblestone path and remove litter. Villagers use the broom more as an instrument to push debris than to pull it forward as those from the States do. As a result, the plastic bristles immediately assume the shape of a tangled mop. Each family possesses a commercial strength pooper-scooper to deploy as required.

Back to my neighbors; the patriarch is in his 80s, while his younger bride approaches her mid-60s. Nikki and I depart for her morning break around 7:45 a.m. The senior chap is in place, push sweeping the leaves and debris which dropped the prior day. Twice per week his wife joins him as she sweeps her flower garden. In Yelapa people sweep the dirt for the same reason they sweep the path---to remove the debris. Now here's where this matrimonial ritual becomes amusing. The gentleman, first on the scene, will have already swept a stretch of the path. His wife advances to the flower bed level, a full three feet or so above the path to produce clouds of dirt, displacing branches, leaves and the odd rotting mango onto the path. She becomes so immersed in her endeavor that she fails to observe her husband working ahead of her. Despite the retention of most aspects of his physical mobility, it is evident that his hearing departed long ago.

As he completes his stretch, he rotates to see his wife, ejecting dirt and debris over the entire path he has just tended. The look on his face speaks volumes---it has to be an ancient version of "WTF?" The verbal exchange that follows escapes my comprehension. I can only guess what transpires. He sets the broom against the wall, marking his spot for the return trip the following morning. Shaking his head as he shuffles, he retires inside. A *futbol* game becomes audible. She finishes sweeping, or should it be brooming the flower bed up to the exact station of her husband's abandoned broom. She looks down the path and shakes her head. The debris remains until her partner of nearly fifty years repeats his task the following morning.

Out to Sea

I am the son of a single parent--mother. Experiencing "guy time" was simply not on my horizon. This activity eludes me until I find myself twenty-two plus years ago becoming part of my wife's family. Since then, my father-in-law, various brothers-in-law and I enjoy "guy time" exchanges. Some are longer than others; some are more one-sided than others but meaningful non-the-less.

Since moving to Yelapa, I find that the majority of my friends are men. This morning presents a period of "guy time." A friend invites me to join him, his brother and his father on a morning fishing jaunt.

Yelapans pay proper homage to their elderly. The father is known to all the villagers. Most greet him with the respectful title: "Don." He understands a goodly amount of English and verbalizes the basics. He is a cancer survivor who now finds his mobility limited. He walks short distances with a cane in each hand or with the use of crutches. Despite all this, he maintains a full-face smile and a host of positive comments about life in general. His humor is dry and punctuated with a sparkle in each eye. He is a joy to engage.

The older of the two sons is serious; focused on the task at hand, a talented storyteller. He is a compendium of oral history passed to him by his grandfather, father and now appended with his own experiences. He is a life-long fisherman and capable captain.

And then there is the younger brother. Despite his rugged muscular physique and manly appearance, he houses the heart and soul of a five year old. He is a gifted clown and entertainer who invariably plants himself into the center of a collection of ladies and works his magic. We'll just leave it at that. His laugh is infectious and despite a voice which sounds vaguely like a skill saw, he frequently breaks into song.

The father and I sit at the rear of the boat, I tend a traditional fishing rig, while he works a hand line. The Captain, his elder son, moves gracefully about the boat, independent of the angle of the floor beneath him. He checks lines and lures, then settles to engage in conversation with his father.

And then there's the younger son. He steers the boat maintaining a safe distance from the coastline. This activity, upon which all of our lives depend, still allows him time to rhythmically beat on the steering wheel, hum loudly and then break into a barely recognizable version of Mario Lanza's "Volare." Ultimately, he stands at the wheel stomping out some folkloric beat intended to divert attention from his vocal delivery; it does not work. The three elders: the father, I and older brother laugh.

During the morning, we catch three fish that the father takes to grill. We laugh, chide each other, and shed a century and a half of accumulated years to return to the carefree times of our youth. It was quality "guy time."

Beef Stew Extraordinaire (*Birria*)

Last night the rains presented with force. At 7:30 a.m. electronic beeps signal the readiness of my carafe of coffee. A moist nose reveals Nikki's readiness for breakfast and a break. The realization is reaffirmed that I am not, and probably have not been for an extended period, in control of my own destiny. It is Sunday; I shalt not dwell.

I tend to Nikki's needs and fill a mug with brown, steaming java. I ease into a chair. The vista before me is spectacular; as if each leaf in the jungle is washed fresh, all roofs are swept and polished and each boulder glistens. The bay reflects an emerald green imparted by the overhanging skies. It is a jaw-dropping vista.

Sunday means *birria* at Ray's Place. For those of you not familiar with this tradition, please refer to an earlier blog entry "Rituals" posted in October. I arrive this morning later than usual. The restaurant is packed. I spy an empty stool at the end of the bar. It is not intended for long-term occupancy; I nod to Ray; he grants approval. My beverage of choice, a bloody Maria, slides within my reach.

Ray and Yuko, the waiters, continuously dart from group to group retrieving drink and *birria* orders. Martina, Caro and Alexa flash through the rooms delivering the required condiments (salt, lime, chopped onion and cilantro, salsa verde and salsa roja). Their return trips bear empty plates, cups and beverage bottles. Violeta, the queen of the kitchen is in consummate control. When the three ladies return to their ready stations, Violeta pivots to issue a flurry of hand signals, all have meaning, and off fly the three again. Ray and Yuko continuously crisscross paths with beverage refills, bowls and plates laden with precious *birria*. It is a symphony of chaos.

There is yet another subtle dynamic in process. I touched briefly on the fact that husbands and wives do not typically eat together. On Sunday morning, many of the menfolk are either out fishing or unable to venture out at the required hour. There are certain two-legged sharks who capitalize on such opportunities. They smile and chat with the women, pinch little girls' cheeks, and even avail themselves to an empty chair for closer engagement. Their smiles are never ending, their laughs are recognizable and collectively they are convinced of the necessary service they provide, or at least offer.

There is a break in the activity level. The event ends for me as it began: a nod to Ray. With a belly full of *birria*, I head for *Casa Azul* to share my Yelapa.

Best of 2013

Last night was the first in four without rain. Sea swells create a seductive rhythm which releases in the lap, lap, lapping on the beach. Only the odd traversing of a *panga* alters my tranquility. AND THEN some S-O-B downstairs activates a Tim Allen grade hammer drill and sets off seismographs from Puerto Vallarta to Manzanillo.

Its mid-morning on a Sunday. The workman responsible for the earlier disruption is spied. I politely inquire as to the status on his project. He signals its completion. Aaah, here I am fat, sassy and ready to write. Let us see where this goes. With three calendar days remaining until the commencement of 2014, I can just slide in this year's Memo's Favorites.

Memo's Favorites for 2013

General
Best:
Yelapa FaceBook Info	YelapaVisitors
WaterTaxi/Captain	La Guerra/Neto
Local attraction	Town Waterfall

Restaurants;
Waterfront Restaurant	Café Bahia
Pozole(Mondaynight)	Ramona's
Riverside Restaurant	El Manguito

Best Restaurant Overall	Ray's Place

Services:
Market	Leticia's
Excursion Guide	MiraMar Excursions
Kayak Rental	Yelapa Kayak Rentals
Electronic Bargain	Prepaid Cell-TelCel

While the categories are massaged slightly, last year's players remain well entrenched. The FaceBook site is new, thanks to Susan Pasko, and offers current information to the Yelapa traveler. The Best Water Taxi/Driver recognizes the performance of one, among many, superb captains. Ray's Place is the new location for Ray, Violeta and Alexa; MiraMar Excursions is a name change from Okley Excursions; lastly, Yelapa Kayak Rentals is now the brand of what was Memo's Kayaks. You'll figure it out. My selections are purely subjective; I urge the potential Yelapa traveler to visit TripAdvisor.com for more objective assessments. If you have questions, contact me via this blog. All of us wish your visit to be tranquil, stress free and worth repeating.

I have not addressed lodging. That decision is based upon a variety of parameters unique to each traveler. Once again, visit TripAdvisor. Yelapa offers something for every pocket book. Do your research. At this point, it might be a great idea to also re-visit an earlier blog posting "Travel Tips 101/102." Pay particular attention to the discussion regarding those with travel limitations.

Happy New Year (January)

New Year's resolution put me in a quandary. I am not one to identify such items despite prodding from a mother, then later from a wife, then an employer and finally the ever popular push by friends. My partner, Diana, will readily acknowledge that I am list averse in general. Resolutions are a type of list. Items such as lose ten pounds, listen to my spouse, and keep my home office clean, are simply rosters of things not done for years and which will remain undone a year from now. When it gets down to any meaningful alteration in behavior, the human animal becomes reptilian. That's to say that the resident organism will make a change when he (masculine pronoun deliberately chosen) decides to do so. No prodding, chiding, cajoling or goading by others will cause an iota of alteration. Let us be honest, we choose a partner because of their positive attributes. The negative ones, we figure we will alter over time-------but we can't. People aren't items you purchase off the rack and take home with the intention of accessorizing. What you have before you, with minor exceptions, is pretty much what cha' gonna get.

Sunshine

An expanded water taxi schedule doubles the arrival of daily visitors. Most dedicate a few hours to Yelapa. Others enter an extended adventure which they share and relive for years. A select few, like us, will make Yelapa their adopted home; contribute to the economy; and actively support others who positively contribute to the welfare of the pueblo.

Strangers on the paths meet and greet. *Motos* (ATVs) involved in commerce await the passing of pedestrians then nod courteously as they resume their travels. For-hire fishing boats depart mid-morning, their hulls full of smiling fisher-people, to return mid-afternoon with their holds full of bounty from the sea. Daily, a dozen or so vessels enter our bay: sailboats, catamarans and high-end charter yachts. Passengers briefly come ashore to sun and fun. They are ferried back to their boats just before dusk to garner the last of daylight before departing. A few boats, like their land counterparts, will spend a day or two within the bay, welcomed warmly by local entrepreneurs.

Restaurants are filled with the gaiety of revelers, old and young alike. Staff greets the travelers with a warm and friendly *"hola."* Each table shares its stories with those of its neighbor. Groups continuously re-organize and reform. By the close of the evening, there is but one great table. This is Yelapa; friendly, warm, inviting, positive.

The previous two "high seasons" have been challenging to local lodging, restaurant owners, and shop keepers. Certainly the worldwide recession played a part, but the largest contributor to the downturn is the perceived security stigma which clouds travel to Mexico. Our Mexican village is no more or less secure than any American village of similar size. Those of you visiting, whether by your actual presence or by reading this blog, are spreading the real word----thank you.

Scattered clouds move in to filter the sunshine. Temperatures remain a little lower so that you enjoy a snack and your chosen libation just a tad more. Smiles are affixed on all the faces I see. We are at peace.

Puerto Vallarta Bound

Yelapans harbor ambivalence toward Puerto Vallarta, our big brother in Banderas Bay. It is the definitive adore-abhor relationship. We adore the department stores, super markets, Pemex stations, marine supply, and even the much maligned American "big box" outlets. On the other hand, we abhor the crowds, the noise, the speed of discourse and the traffic while knowing full-well that these are the very requisites for sustaining the opportunities we adore. Alas, even in paradise befuddlement abounds.

On Monday, I make such a trip. THE plan consists of boarding the 8:30 a.m. ish water taxi, arriving at Los Muertos Pier around 9:45 a.m., stopping at the ATM and catching a bus to my first errand. Well, things do not always go according to plan. Around 8:15 a.m. the skies darken and a gentle rain begins to fall. No problem, I re-work THE plan to the 9:30 a.m. taxi. On approaching the pier, I encounter several like-planning types who in the aggregate constitute a full taxi. Following a brief pause in Quimixto, plus a stop in Boca de Tamatlan, we arrive in Vallarta near 11 a.m.

My feet kick into auto-walk mode and in a few moments I stand in front of the ATMs at Banorte. There is a line of tourists, all set to load their pockets with cash and shop, shop, shop. You gotta love 'em (and thank you for coming). My turn arrives and I enter the booth. There is a beep-beep-beep emitted by the machine. A quick scan identifies that the preceding patron neglected to extract his bank card. Now this is heady stuff, the piece of plastic residing in my palm could define bliss or devastation for the remainder of this chap's visit. The card is conveyed to a gentleman in a suit sitting behind a desk, inside the bank. We exchange smiles.

A two minute walk and I arrive at the bus hub in the *Zona Romantica*. The fare is seven pesos. That's a deal! A raised arm signals my wish to board. The bus stops, door opens, following a quick verification of my destination, I ascend the stairs, pay my fare, receive my receipt and exchange smiles. After twenty minutes or so, my destination appears. I exit, tell the driver "thank you" and he responds with "have a good day." I am one of several hundred people to whom he will extend an identical comment.

My errands complete, I hail a taxi and return to Los Muertos Pier. Inside the cab, the driver asks the usual question, "are you going to Yelapa?" I proudly disclose that I live there. He continues with sincere inquiries. His chosen route zig-zags through the cobble stones of Old Town. We pass the large open space on the *Malecón* where entertainers congregate. I spy two Tourist Police in their spotless, starched white uniforms attempting to carry on a conversation. Each maneuvers a Segway; the resulting syncopated ballet is amusing to say the least. My smile greets them as we motor past. I arrive at the pier; pay, tip and express appreciation. My efforts are met with a sincere response. We smile.

Thirty minutes remain until the "scheduled" departure to Yelapa. The pier is laden with visitors speaking a host of languages. Children of all ages dart about. Two Tourist Police on foot sprint about the pier with uncharacteristic intensity. A band of boys is utilizing the lower pier structure as their personal diving platform. The resulting show is reminiscent of the Keystone Cops. The boys swim to one area and scream, the police run to that location. The boys disappear underwater to reappear at another site. They make loud noises again, the police pursue, etc. etc. etc. The entire pier population is in stitches. The Tourist Police ultimately realize the doomed nature of their pursuit and strategically withdraw. Their efforts draw applause.

Our water taxi pulls into Yelapa Bay just

prior to 3 p.m. The tide has retreated so that the earth tones of the beach greet the incoming traveler. It occurs to me that the main beach is shaped like a huge smile. How special is that? It is the perfect ending to a great day; one of many smiles. Thank you, Puerto Vallarta.

Bits-n-Bobs

It is a diverse week in Yelapa. Four spectacular sunny days, follow a gray intruder, another sunny fellow and lastly intermittent grey-sunny-clear-sprinkles. I am totally confused, perhaps my threshold is lower than most. Our little bay provides shelter to a diverse collage of visitors. Early on a young hump-back whale passes deep into Yelapa Bay to befriend a sailboat at anchor. The onboard canine sounds the alert. The owners, perhaps enjoying an early morning cup of java, fail to heed the call. Those of us observing the event wonder if this might not be the adolescent born two years prior just off the southern point of our bay. Following the birth, mother and charge remain in that secure site for nearly a week, all in front of ogling eyes.

We also provide safe harbor to seven world-class sailboats. These are not the casual day sailing vessels which inhabit the marinas *al norte*. These are serious sailors aboard beautiful boats equipped with solar panels, wind turbines and long range communication equipment. These are forty to fifty foot vessels commanded by men and women who appear well-seasoned at their task and mature in their years. They treat their surrounds and their hosts with respect. Their departures are as skilled and silent as their arrivals.

On a darker side, two outboard motors are stolen from local *pangas* during the night. Conversation surfaces regarding re-installing a high intensity light to oversee the bay at night. A year back, one is installed but following a two week engagement is removed amid complaints from residents who feel the light to be intrusive. I sense this activity, removing and redeploying of marine assets, is a fairly fluid one among the seaside villages of Banderas Bay. Boats, engines, *motos*, scooters, jet skis, etc. are bought and sold for cash. Few questions are asked; ownership documentation may not be an issue. Such transactions are a fact of life.

Unplugged

Some of my readers recall life BPC (before personal computers). My generation utilized the twelve page calendar as well as the Day Runner. Both grant Type A personalities an opportunity to inscribe current and future endeavors. Undoubtedly, these devices now occupy some wooden drawer in the bowels of the Smithsonian Institute.

Mid-morning, I receive a phone call from a friend. He proclaims "we need to talk about business." I'm good, second cup of coffee in hand, most cylinders are firing. He states that his wife's laptop died and she wishes to borrow mine, for the better part of four days (9a.m. to 5p.m.). I can have the item at night. I reply "no problem."

Before participating in this laptop loan program, my computer habits are chronicled as follows: sweep thru email during second cup of coffee; check news, check blog stats, open Face Book. Leave FB open to hear notifications of "like" or "comment" or "share". Wash the morning dishes while attempting to ignore FB notifications. Check the FB notifications, sweep email accounts again, check stats on my blog, and check two other blogs to read latest postings. Make one of three lunch options: 1) *Pacifico*-guacamole; 2) Pacifico-Mexican seasoned peanuts; or 3) the low-calorie version, just a *Pacifico*. Return to laptop and repeat the morning cycle.

At 2:30 p.m. sharp; I open Skype, alter my status to "Do not disturb" and engage in my siesta. Back on the move at 4p.m. sweep accounts, check stats, and scan worldly events. Feed Nikki, feed me, either in-house or out-of-house, Skype the wife, pull up Netflix and retire for the evening after making coffee for the following morning. This is my life. For the next ninety-six hours, everything between my second cup of coffee and feed Nikki vanishes. (Except lunch with my good friend *Señor Pacifico*)

What occurs during this now vacuous eight hour block? ? ? ? ? ? I retrieve a National Geographic book on photography that I had not touched in eight weeks; I give the house a thorough cleaning. I give Nikki a bath, trim her nails and medicate her skin; I practice my guitar for the first time in five months; I put my camera in my pocket whenever I depart and photograph (or do people say "pix?") scenes which complement the children's series I am writing. I experience the liberation of Andy Dufresne in ShawShank Redemption. (ok, that's a bit over the top) Besides, didn't he go to Zihuatanejo?

Much is published regarding establishing home No Device Zones or No Device Times. This great French video clip poignantly addresses this issue:

(http://www.youtube.com/embed/V_gOZD WQj3Q?rel=0).

Give it some thought. Who knows what you

might discover? "Don't cost nothing." (John Belushi, Animal House)

To and Fro

Today, three of our friends return for a month. Yelapa serves as their getaway, a mental and physical haven. Two of this group reside in Fairbanks, Alaska. They encounter snow and temperatures in the -30s (F). As they both embrace their chronological autumns, such encounters become less and less attractive. Chloe, their Scottie, now revels in her daily romp on the beach.

The third returnee, climbed on a plane at Chicago's O'Hare Airport, morning temperature -21 (F) and should have Yelapa sand in her toes by afternoon. Chicago experiences brutal cold fronts which drive temperatures to nearly -40 (F). Yet another storm moves in as I write. She will make her way thirty minutes up river, to a home she has lovingly appointed and leave the door open to permit the latest brood of chicks to pay their respects.

For the next thirty days, we all meet, greet, eat, drink and kayak. Each individual will carve out pockets of time to perform packets of work. The balance will be devoted to spontaneity. Our foursome will expand to a fivesome with the return of my wife. Her full time duties as Nanny-Granny are passed temporarily to a sister. When that occurs, my life will be better. Once she arrives, the resident four will rehash the same stories already conveyed, return to the same restaurants already visited and sip our way through the same libations we know so well.

Birthday Party

Yelapans require no excuse to celebrate. However, when a marriage merges with the birthdays of the bride and groom, it is a Mexican *cause celebre*. The celebration site is up river at the home of the groom's parents. I am close with this entire family, and look forward to the event .

First, I need to convey local social norms. There is never a guest list. Neighbors, friends, visitors and casual passers-by are all welcomed, fed and libated. Beverage coolers are scattered across the site. Bar-b-que chicken and steak, rice, frijoles, homemade salsas and tortillas are present. The scene is punctuated with a portable stereo system including jumbo speakers.

The gender dynamics mirror those of a stateside seventh-grade dance; men on one side of the festive arena while the women occupy the opposing side. The groom serves the gentlemen, the bride attends to the ladies.

As the evening progresses, two dynamics evolve: initially, the head count grows from thirty to well over fifty; a collection of *futbol* (soccer) fans relocates to the living room flat screen. This re-positioning of males is hardly noticed. As the evening progresses, the volume on the stereo increases, the volume from the now highly animated male discussions increases. An inverse reaction occurs with the women. Their conversations have traveled their course and now attention is drawn to the antics of their respective mates. They respond with muted chortles and head shaking.

As departure time approaches, I express my appreciation to the bride and groom, the parents of the groom and bid *"buenas noches"* to the balance. It is an evening with brilliant stars. I pass and greet others on the path. It is a good night to be a Yelapan.

Boxco

This business (Costco) enjoys a love affair with the American people since its founding in 1983. The opportunity to garner discounts on virtually every purchase, regardless of its necessity, resides within the helix of the shopping public's DNA. According to Wikipedia, Costco is now the second largest domestic

(USA) retailer with a total of 632 outlets in 8 countries including 33 in Mexico. Yes, there is one in Puerto Vallarta. Despite its size, the company acts in a responsible manner. Just in passing, the largest domestic (USA) retailer—Walmart "enjoys" no such fame.

Remember when a trip to Costco meant total purchases of $100, and then it jumped to $250 and now—who knows? Men enter to be seduced by the latest electronics. A right turn beckons toward rows of appliances, tools, athletic equipment, automotive accessories etc. etc. etc. We are doomed. Think Ahab and the Great White Whale. Ok, you know the drill.

Mexican Costco is more dangerous. Take all the above items, throw them into your basket and march through the checkout line. Naturally, your reference point is that Costco is the greatest of all discount houses on the planet, well, in Mexico maybe not so much. All those prices you see on the shelves will increase at checkout time by a whopping 16% for IVA. This is the Mexican version of VAT or value added tax. Chances are you won't notice it, as you extract multiple 500 peso bills or your credit card (yes, Costco Mexico does accept credit cards) from your wallet.

The Mexican government requires all American box stores (Home Depot,

Walmart/Sam's Club, Costco, Office Depot, Staples) to impose this tax while local super markets do not. Stores like Mega and Soriano are giant grocery stories with electronics departments, appliances, and nearly everything offered by Costco. My point here is to alert the traveler that you may want to do some price shopping.

I shop Costco once a week for wine, tequila, coffee, tuna and the odd jug of desiccant. My march past the cashier is generally followed by lunch. All the usual suspects are offered: hot dogs, package salads, chicken rolls and pizza. I order two hot dogs plus my free drink and proceed to the condiment area. Awaiting me are onions, mustard, ketchup plus the regional staple---jalapeños. I craft my feast and select a seat. I fail to understood why you have umbrellas indoors at a food court? Are there ultra-violet ray emitting overhead lights?

After lunch, I pass the Receipt Review Technician and exit. I hail a cab to the bus to Boca or directly to Los Muertos Pier. Having departed Yelapa at 8:30am ish, I open my door to *Casa Azul* and greet Nikki at roughly 12:30. Sometime that afternoon, I will unpack my treasures; there is no rush.

Kids (February)

Those who grew up (whatever that means) during the 1950s, 60s or even the 70s enjoyed a window in United States history that may never exist again. Youth was defined by blocks of time just to be a kid. I recall untold hours spent riding my bike over dirt mounds or city streets, off to the public pool, climbing trees, chasing lizards, having dirt clod battles, investigating the giant concrete culverts at the new freeway site, shooting archery in my front yard, cruising Park Central Mall, watching the first episode of The Mickey Mouse Club (damn, Annette was gorgeous), participating as a crossing guard at Heard Elementary School, taking the bus downtown to the YMCA twice a week, and finally spending a disproportionate amount of time in the office of Mr. Krauss, the school principal. Corporal punishment was alive and applied.

Our parent's primary political concern was "the bomb." We were dead center of the Cold War. Some folks built fallout shelters. I excavated a bath tub sized area in the back yard as my contribution to our family's tenuous security. Despite all of the freedom that surrounded us, we were not free-range. Our parents continued to mete out discipline when we messed up. We knew when it was coming, we knew what it would be, we expected it, accepted it and moved on.

My mother's preferred disciplinary tool was "grounding," generally a month at a whack! I spent half my high school career under house arrest. In contrast, today's youth are either hyper-scheduled (dance, sports, swim, cheer, gymnastics, body building, reading club, private tutoring, junior militia, etc. etc. etc.) or they assume a sedentary posture to devote hours among electronic devices. They no longer are required to think at all much less think critically. Their lives unfold with others who think at them. Hence when the need for discipline arises, it deteriorates into an exercise executed by those who are as inept at delivering it as their charges are at receiving it. Enough said.

Laughter arises from the beach. A quick glance identifies four boys romping in a trough created by the Tuito River cutting through the sand bar and emptying into the bay. They roll, dive, squeal, splash, scream, and laugh for the better part of three hours. A trip through the chute lasts half a minute. Once complete, they run back to travel again and again and again. They are kids being kids. A smile grows across this wrinkled face.

Of the ten or so activities identified in the opening paragraph, virtually none of them would be allowable today. Progeny are chauffeured to their friends houses; construction sites are fenced and guarded; lizards are visited at the Reptile House of some zoo; archery anywhere on the premises would violate the neighborhood CC&Rs; homes have pools installed which are rarely used; private contractors now provide crossing guard services; the original Mickey Mouse Club wound down by 1960; ask a kid today to take a bus—you know what type of look that would generate; and corporal punishment—we cannot begin to walk down that path.

My hope is that children today are still sent the principal's office. My fear is that they are sent by inept classroom instructors to a senior inept administrative disciplinarian who then calls the parents to discuss a concept about which they (the parent and the administrator) know little or nothing. Remember when it was fun to be a kid? Find a raggedy pair of shorts, a t-shirt, a pair of flip-flops and bring them to Yelapa. Find the kid you used to be.

The Plumber

Today, I need a plumber. There is one chap I prefer, his name is Nacho (short of Ignacio). I spoke with him two days ago and set a tentative appointment for Monday morning. Monday morning comes and goes, no Nacho. The "ish" factor activates. Tuesday morning, he appears tools in hand.

I discuss with him in rather graphic detail that my continued manhood is at risk if this problem is not resolved prior to my wife's return on Friday. He nods in consummate understanding. Now Nacho is somewhat unique, even in Yelapa; he does not own a cell phone. He is available through his home number, a landline. If he has departed for the day, then one must leave a message. It is a simple yet simultaneously brilliant strategy. He cannot be disturbed or located once he departs.

Nacho sets to work. Nikki growls disenchantment from her crated captivity. I work on the computer. Numerous sighs, groans, and phrases exit the bathroom. He emerges, alerts me to his departure and disappears for nearly an hour. Nacho re-appears and returns to work. Ten minutes later he beckons. I am told that the commode is incorrectly installed. (This isn't starting off well). He discloses two options: 1) create a concrete lip and base upon which the commode will now sit—hopefully this will seal the leak; 2) knock out the tile from the wall behind and move the toilet back the required distance. I choose option number one. He nods; as he departs he states "I'll return between five and six this evening to check on things."

Siesta completed, I arise. Five o'clock ticks away, followed by five thirty. At 5:59pm exactly, there is a knock on my front door. Nacho enters; passes to the area of concern; grunts approval and declares *"todo bien"* (all is well). My bill for an hour's work, plus a return trip; 200 pesos ($17.50 USD).

My wife will never know—unless she reads this post. Nacho departs stating that my manhood should remain intact. I express my appreciation.

Dogs

There is an estimated 1.85 dogs for every man, woman and child in Yelapa. I avoid the verb "own" since it is impossible to tell who actually cares for, tends to or dare I say "owns" a particular dog. No leash law exists so what leashes are employed typically belong to visitors. Some people carry an unattached leash. I never understand what that accomplishes either for the person or their animal.

I own a dog, Nikki, an English Shepherd. We depart *Casa Azul* twice daily to attend to her needs. She is leashed prior to departing. The tether is removed once we re-enter the front door. The family below me "owns" three medium-sized dogs. There were four, but alas the old Chihuahua died. The remaining three, like all their Yelapan cousins, roam free throughout their territory. Each of them emits a loud if not threatening chorus of barks at passing mules, *motos* (quads), scooters and pedestrians. I have initiated a one-man campaign to express my disenchantment. In all honesty, several of the household members now make token attempts to quiet these three.

I am not a vengeful person, but last night vengeance was mine. The youngest of the three canines, which also exhibits the loudest bark and behaves in the most aggressive manner, was sprayed by a skunk. Now Mexican skunks spray a similarly acrid scent yet it is slightly different; perhaps occasioned by a diet of papaya leaves and poblano chili. Once the incident occurs, the dog rockets through the open door of the "owners" dwelling. All hell breaks loose. The dog is corralled, restrained and tethered to a tree where it vocalizes its displeasure.

The resident family spends the ensuing three hours on the street in front of their abode, bidding *"buenas noches"* to polite travelers who extract their faces from protective hoodies as they pass. Fortunately, the prevailing breeze is such that *Casa Azul* is upwind. By 11:30 pm, I doze off to the shuffle of foot traffic followed by fatigued voices repeating *"buenas noches."*

(Yes Virginia, there is a Santa Claus.)

Kayak versus Horse

In Yelapa, kayaks and horses transport people and the occasional limited quantity of goods. However, as the operator of Yelapa Kayak Rentals, it is abundantly clear to me that kayaks offer distinct advantages over their four-footed competitors. Here are but a few:

1. Kayaks require limited storage, can be stacked on top of each other or carried on top of your car.
2. You need not care (medically) nor feed nor clean up after a kayak.
3. While kayaking, you are not required to follow the person in front of you. This enhances your view dramatically.
4. Kayaks do not stop to take a dump or emit clouds of lung collapsing gas.
5. Kayaks do not need to be chased, bridled or saddled before mounting.
6. No specialty clothing is required. As a matter of fact, minimal clothing is expected.
7. As you pivot toward the starting point with a kayak, it does not suddenly bolt for the beach.
8. After kayaking, no one will ever tell you

that you smell like a horse.
9. While it is possible to fall out of a kayak, it will never bite nor buck you.

Rarely has an argument been laid out more coherently.

Rhythm

At the core of life lies the principle of rhythm. Obvious inclusions: seasons, tides, migration, sunrise/sunset, lunar phases, earth's trip around the sun and the plethora of constellations observed along the route, etc. Man, in his endeavor to imitate and refine nature, invented the clock to identify increments such as second, minute and hour. He/she was then forced to craft labels for the recurring nature of successive blocks of twenty-four hours, hence, our now existent days of the week. I am uncertain as to why only seven such blocks result. Perchance this number depicts the quantity of firewood which could be stored in a cave, or the number of days you wear your toga before it requires washing.

During another increment labeled "vacation," one turns to one's travel partner and utters, "I've lost all track of time. I don't know what day it is." It is at this juncture that our reptilian brain re-engages. We strip away the man-made labels of time and react to the primitive cycles of our cave dwelling ancestors. When the outside elements are harsh; you seek shelter. When your body requires food or drink; you search for satisfaction. When a potential mate wonders by, you make short grunting noises, offer food and beverage, then retreat to share the interior of your extensive real estate holdings. The approach changes little over the past ten thousand years.

In Yelapa, natural cycles rule. We experience basically two seasons separated by a forty-five day transition period. Beginning in November and continuing through April, we embrace the season of Drop Dead Gorgeous. May follows and ushers a heat/humidity transition dragging us into June. Once there, we launch into raging humidity, monsoonal rains, and oppressive temperatures. This is the season we refer to as The Great Oppression. Locals hunker down, while ex-pats get the hell out of Dodge (Yelapa).

As I write this piece, I am engulfed by the rhythms of a chop-saw grinding its way through one inch square pieces of metal. The tool accelerates to a high pitch, decreases as it encounters resistance, nearly dies only to re-accelerate at the final instant. This is not one of nature's cycles; it belongs to man. Alas, it is silent once more. Perhaps, my fellow reptiles have ambled off to seek satisfaction of the rhythms of sustenance, or to make short grunting noises.

Morning

My morning in Yelapa commences following five electronic beeps from my coffee maker. That signals Nikki to beat her tail against the bed frame until my hand reaches through the netting and plants atop her head. This is our ritual seven days a week. By the time my feet fit into flip-flops, the birds have welcomed the new morn for over an hour. The roosters tuned up at 3:30 a.m. Nikki is fed, watered, and walked. We return 8ish; I settle into my chair for the first cup of coffee.

Yelapa is the year-round home to twenty or so Great Frigate birds. As their name implies, these are large birds three feet in length and with a v-angled wing-span of nearly seven feet. Their design has been the inspiration for more than one piece of aerial military hardware. They cruise and climb effortlessly for hours almost disappearing from sight. The females, who display a white penguin-syle blaze, are larger than the males.

Before the sun creeps up the ridge line, a lone female frigate bird appears from up the Tuito River and glides the perimeter of Yelapa Bay. I paddle this route daily in my kayak. It consumes nearly an hour of my time while the frigate bird navigates the distance in a few moments. She pivots into the center of the bay, vectors 180 degrees and retires up river. The bay is now open. Nearly a dozen hours hence the sun descends the ridge line; an identical, if not the same, female frigate bird repeats the ritual. There are no other birds in the sky; she circles, draws a radius to the center and returns up river. The bay is closed. In the morning, I bid her *"buenas dias"* with a steaming cup of rich coffee. Each evening, I raise a glass of wine in wonderment.

Puzzlement

Yelapa is ripe with rituals and rhythms. A few puzzle me. Each morning, I observe workers at the beach restaurants engaged in raking the sand. My confusion arises from the fact that twice daily, high tides level the sand and impart a moist, reflective appearance. This polished state is then altered by rakers etching half-inch deep parallel lines across their assigned frontage. This quasi-meditative effect lingers until the arrival of the first humine or canine who blindly violates the artwork.

My quandary continues. The tides deposit rows of dark organic material. Each raker meticulously creates piles of this debris. A shovel excavates a hole and the material is deposited. These receptacles reside ten feet from the existing water line. High tides course the water a minimum of fifteen feet onto the beach. Therefore, the contents of each receptacle are revealed, return to the sea to be recast upon the shore. This all occurs within the ensuing twelve hours, always has always will.

The next morning, you guessed it, the Yelapa Raking Team reconvenes to further hone their skills. It is a puzzlement!

Yelapa Recipes (March)

If you landed here expecting to discover the detailed recipes of the greatest offerings from each of Yelapa's dozen restaurants, then I have taunted you and will taunt you again. Recipes are fiercely guarded. Such has been the case for generations. Daughters and grand-daughters learn from ancient hands and agile minds. Virtually all ingredients are fresh.

Let us explore two "creations". The first is *"café de olla"* or simply coffee from the urn. Mexico cultivates a variety of coffees. Each household selects its preferred bean/blend. This hot morning beverage is made with purified water, freshly ground coffee, and an assortment of secret ingredients. It then simmers slowly on the stove in a terra cotta pot (*olla*). Some restaurants offer both *"café de maquina"* (electric coffee maker) and *"café de olla."* Try the later. A few words of caution: taste the beverage before adding cream and sugar; and avoid swirling or tipping the cup upside down to get the last drop.

The second of the two creations is *"salsa Mexicana,"* some of you know it as *"pico de gallo"* or *"casera"* salsa. This is the quintessential Mexican salsa (it displays the colors of the national flag) made from chopped tomatoes, white onions, cilantro and green chilies. Every morning pathways palpitate with rapid chopping. It is an indication that fresh salsa is being crafted. Two suggestions: first, try a small amount in advance of slathering it all over your meal. Second, this salsa only appears on the table in the morning. It is considered inappropriate to utilize *"salsa Mexicana"* on a dinner selection—something akin to putting ketchup on your mahi-mahi.

Traveling invites opportunities for gastronomic exploration. When visiting Yelapa, discard everything you thought you knew about "Mexican" food. Push beyond your comfort zone. Once you do, you will be exposed to sights, smells and tastes you never dreamed possible. *Buen Provecho!!*

Diversity

Gaze into any face of Yelapa. Each is a caricature, a piece of art, a multi-generational storybook. Skin tones run the gamut of pale white to deep brown. Distinct features are discernible within each of the four original families. There are short ones, tall ones, fat ones, skinny ones. Our village includes men dedicated to continuous sacrifices to their patron saints, *Santa Corona, San Pacifico* or *Santa Tequila.* There are a few, who enhance their earnings through the sale of illegal substances. From time to time, there is a village thief. Whenever something is stolen, the affected party, or their landlord, knows where to go. If the event is serious, the police are summoned and the individual is incarcerated, again. We have one elderly beggar lady. Her walking stick's tap-tap-tap announces her approach. There is a mentally challenged adult. She bothers no one, and asks for nothing. She periodically rests on various benches throughout the village. And lastly, we even have a bully (no not the guy with the boat) who like Punxsutawney Phil exits self-imposed exile to pitch her latest barrel of bile.

In addition to the individuals mentioned above are countless hard working laborers, doctors, craftsmen, water taxi captains, fishing boat captains, teachers, students, market operators, waiters, cooks, guides, housekeepers, gardeners, kayak rental chaps, fresh anything (cheese, fruit, chicken, bread, fish) vendors, restaurateurs, lodging managers, baggage transporters AND the two internationally renowned Yelapa Pie Ladies. We are a village of diversity.

Many visitors reside in compounds of sameness. It is their personal choice. Others thrive amongst diverse humans who wave hello, call out from their door way or simply smile. They are neither tall nor short, slender nor fat, pale nor dark; they are simply human.

Vitamin K (Kayak)

Remember the last time you woke up and everything just clicked? This morning begins with Nikki's muzzle on the bedside, her tail pounds out some primitive pattern on the adjacent plastic tub. The microwave beams 7:00 a.m. Breakfast and a walk for N takes us past our favorite juice stand and then into the jungle. So far so good. N and I return to a steeping pot of rich coffee and our morning play time. I'm now ready for the world's best smoothie: papaya, pineapple, banana, granola, honey, Katy yogurt and chia seeds. The blender kicks into puree and the entire *casita* quivers. I love it. Two tumblers later, I am sated.

I depart *Casa Azul*, around 10 a.m. to link up with kayak clients. I set up a single yak. A half hour past the reservation time, I launch. The water is crystal clear. It yields that "see forever" look. My submersible camera rests at the ready. Several schools of blue-runners dart past, puffer fish flap calmly. I juggle paddle and camera, frequently confusing the two. Finally, I am poised with the right instrument submerged to produce the desired effect. Since I remain atop my yak, I have no idea in what direction the camera is pointing. I note the influx of small jellyfish. They are intriguing in their complexity. I thrust the camera into the water.

A spotted eagle ray glides beneath me. My excitement produces neither camera nor results. I paddle on towards The Point. Swells increase but clarity remains. A school of bonita surround me, yellow dorsal fins knife the surface, and then rocket past.

I pivot the yak and spot the ray. A smaller one swims alongside. This time, I know the drill. Camera thrust into the water and pointed, let it be, let it be, please!

It is all about size!

Having peered into Yelapa Bay for two and a half years, I ogle, research and fantasize over dozens of luxury yachts, sailboats and catamarans.

These vessels are diverse and embody varying attitudes about their relationship with sea. Motor yachts demand your respect as a result of sheer size and mammoth horsepower. The presence of that power reverberates throughout Yelapa Bay. The blasting of air horns dislodges mangos from trees and causes coronary distress in iguanas. Bows display names which assert the yacht's aggression over the sea: Invader, Negotiator, or a less than subtle reference to size; Mama Mia. Their lengths respectively are: 168', 57', and 120'. Any seaman will tell you that there is nothing shabby about a 57' craft. On its own, the Negotiator appears formidable in our bay, right up to the moment when one of the "big boys" arrives. At that point, it strategically withdraws. It is all about size.

Sailboats are the antithesis of the power yacht. Historically, they harken to long ago days of exploration, skirmishes and ultimately a co-existence. The interaction is defined by hard work and mutual respect. Typically their names reflect a whimsical approach to their presence: Scuttlebutt, Vitamin Sea or Nauti Girl.

Catamarans, my personal favorites, occupy a unique space. Under sail, they appear to take flight rather than be bound to the sea. When moored in our bay, they offer the open play space of a forward trampoline; a feature distinct unto themselves. Such names as Humu Humu (a mythical Hawaiian bird), Star Chaser, or Segue reflect their status as both drawn to the wind while affixed to the sea. Frequently they travel in clusters.

A single category remains; no it is not the humble kayak. It is the common panga. Immensely seaworthy, these boats are the life blood of isolated coastal villages around the world. Yelapa is home to perhaps fifty such vessels. Virtually all bear the name of the owner's first daughter: Diana, Alexandra, Violeta, Alexa, Yuri, Yesenia, Irena, Norma or Erika. Their naming acknowledges it was from the sea that we gained life. The giving back, via the *panga's* name, returns to the sea the value of that earlier gift. It is a romantic notion, is it not?

This week's news (April)

Patchy clouds glide on gentle breezes. This morning at 2:00 a.m., Mexico crossed into day light savings. Early attendance at Ray's

Place for *birria* is sparse, but will enjoy a late morning surge as eyes open and feet find flip-flops. Few villagers wear watches. Across the bay, froth bathes and then recedes from the eastern shoreline. Sea swells enter from due west. Water taxi passage out will be smooth, but the return is bound to bounce. Nature rules in Yelapa, not the rotating hands on a dial.

Aline and Bill return from Santa Barbara; Erin arrives Tuesday having endured Chicago's winter from hell; Tamara and John will shortly jet away from Fairbanks. There will be much eating, drinking and laughter; there always is. Alas, for those of you curious about my dear wife, she remains engaged as the care provider for the granddaughter Our orbits will intersect late July.

The end of April registers a reduction in visitor traffic. A trickle trails into June. Once the rains arrive, a few Mexican nationals and Americans families venture across Banderas Bay. They will experience a quiet village. Locals will begin the six month rationing of precious resources: time and money. *Pangas*, white bellies up, populate the beach awaiting seasonal repairs and repainting. Construction greets each morning and drones until sunset. Repairs proceed on rental units or an expansion of the family home. It is a time of renewal. (That is code for noise, humidity and heat.) Any down time is spent on a friend's *panga* fishing. Summer rains bring in the big fish: tuna, dorado, red snapper. Freezers must be filled.

Our English shepherd, Nikki and I plan a July departure to San Diego. It is our time for renewal. (Same word, different code. This implies periodic cycling amongst the in-laws and re-establishing tenuous truces with canine cousins.) For the past year or so, I have written a series of dual language, English and Spanish, books for children. Each book portrays a real boy's real adventure in Yelapa. By November 1, my goal is to have the first adventures ready for e-publishing. The intended audience, either English or Spanish, ranges from the pre-reader thru second grade. The illustrator is my partner/mate Dianne. The rich watercolors emerge from photographs of local scenery. Collectively, they become a visual collage for future visitors.

Reflections

It seems mind boggling (or is it blogging?) that one and a half years ago Yelapa Memo, the blog, was created. My focus remains the sharing of village life. Since that October morn, eighty-one postings have garnered nearly 6500 visits from more than a dozen countries. To the eighty-five of you who read the first posting *"Viva"* and have continued with me, your charter blogger cards should appear in your email boxes shortly.

We are also mid-point in our rental of *Casa Azul*. The view through our bay window is no less hypnotic today than it was the first time we entered. Hours are invested peering through this giant screen saver as something slowly approaches while another something slowly departs.

Further reflection reminds me that I am one renewal away from achieving permanent resident (not citizenship) status in Mexico. It amuses me that I carry a green card issued by the Mexican government. Americans are welcomed to reside, albeit there are requirements, in Mexico. Mexicans are unwelcome to reside in the United States.

A Day in the Bay

Fact: On balance, the villagers in Yelapa are hard-working, warm and welcoming people.
Fact: Almost daily, luxury yachts venture to Yelapa, spend time and then de part.
Fact: During five months of each calendar year, Yelapa is one of the most beautiful places on earth.
Therefore: I live in a beautiful place, surrounded by warm people and visited by those with immense wealth, right?

Nothing is manufactured in Yelapa. Long ago, villagers engaged in fishing. Then they harvested coconut oil from coconut palms. Now, the only "industry" is tourism; despite the numerous travel books which continue to depict us as "a romantic fishing village." Perhaps that sells better than stating "a romantic tourist village." Tourism affords much of the population five months to earn a year's pay. By May 1, most restaurants close, many lodging sites seal up, and the vast majority of pale faces exit. Tourism, unlike the seasonal monsoons, slows to a sprinkle. Young males seek work on construction projects.

The other afternoon, an eighty-foot luxury yacht pulls into Yelapa Bay and drops anchor. A quick internet search identifies ten or so similar yachts on the world market with prices ranging from $1.2 to $2.6 million dollars. After observing this boat intermittently for the next hour, two bits of information become evident. Initially, there appears to be a crew of four. They are easily identifiable by their matching polo shirts and shorts. Secondly, the yacht is the private domicile of one couple. They are bronze, handsome and mature chronologically. They move among the various platforms with grace. As the sun sets, the pair retires to the after deck to enjoy wine, snacks and ultimately dinner. Sometime around 10:30 p.m., I hear an anchor chain retracting. Two engines awaken to push the vessel quietly onward. The yacht departs our little bay leaving no trace of its visit. They are the perfect guests. I wonder if they consider Yelapa the perfect host.

Holy Week

The morning sun shines upon a vacant beach, sailboats waggle their masts as Frigate Birds circle overhead, the tide is out. Nothing different from that which has occurred for millennia. Now, I could just leave it at that but . . . . I won't.

Today hails the conclusion of the most celebrated seventy-two hours in Christendom. Commencing with Good Friday and culminating with Easter Sunday, Christians worldwide celebrate the holiest of holies. Here in Yelapa, the most conspicuous of the faithful dawn special attire, head gear and reading material. They assume grave and somber faces set on the shelf a year ago. The moderately faithful schlepp coolers full of refreshments to enjoy the last getaway before the oppressive heat arrives. Those of us residing in the lowest stanine on the Faithful Scale maneuver thru/around/past the religious huddled masses who occupy the center ninety-eight percent of all pathways. What do you say to someone who suddenly arises from a path-side shrine, pivots directly in front of you and then glances up. "Good morning", "how are you", or "did you have a pleasant shrine time?" I am never sure.

Alas, our little village returns to its former self. Parents, grandparents and countless children pile into *pangas* that ferried them on Friday. Ice chests once full are empty. The incidence of giant plastic bags is less, signaling they contained clothing or gifts for local relatives. The entire family occupies the beach and awaits the *panga*. Once those departing are safely onboard, those ashore commence waving like two legged palm frowns. This entire ritual will play out again in the coming year. It always has.

Bring out your dead!

Casa Azul occupies the fourth floor of a large concrete block building. The remaining three levels house a clan of the largest family in Yelapa. On any given day, there are great-grandparents, grandparents, sons, daughters and a collection of children. None has the remotest awareness regarding noise creation, sustaination, avoidation or abatation (work with me). Wrought iron doors are flung open/shut at warp speed two dozen times per day. Children in steel-toed flip flops run free-range within the building. Lastly, a trio of canines periodically pierces the peacefulness.

It is a cacophony of harmonic discord. Intermittently, I have discretely introduced the concept that "less is better." We actually seemed to be making progress.

Today, "the family" took it to a whole new level. A tempest of teenagers bursts onto the path armed with a drum, cow bell, tambourine, and bugle. Each spontaneously breaks into unbridled, independent creativity. For those within a hundred meters in either direction, the collective dissonance is tantamount to playing a Miles Davis compact disc in reverse.

Upon further research, I determine that this roaming band is touring the village offering their talents (???) to extricate spirits during Holy Week. For some fee based upon square footage and estimated number of ill-spirits, this group will enter your domicile drums ra-ta-tat-ting, cow bells clunking, tambourines tinkling, and one bugle blowing. The resulting melodious (???) mayhem is capable of turning concrete grout into dust within thirty seconds. Just in passing, they re-extricate the domicile below me three times.

Happy Days are Here Again! (May)

Recall the scene in John Huston's classic film *The Night of the Iguana*, where the pathetic group of church women travels through Mexico on a dilapidated bus? Their delusional leader frequently cajoles the group into iterations of the above captioned song. The women sing against the backdrop of oppressive heat, sweat and grit plus the deafening mechanical groans of a vehicle near death. The juxtaposition is brilliant.

In Yelapa, we have two reasons to offer our voices in support of Huston's traumatized travelers. Yesterday afternoon at 2:00 p.m. (CST) the "feels like" temperature registers 90s F. The humidity reaches 70%. Temps throughout this week are expected to nudge further northward (up) by another degree or two. Recall the expression of being able to fry an egg on the sidewalk? Here in Yelapa, you can poach one. Summer arrives/lands/befalls/bursts forth; pick one. It remains until late October, punctuated with monsoonal rains beginning mid-June. The jungle erupts into countless shades of green, the crabs migrate, game fish of all nature enter Banderas Bay and streams, creeks and rivers flow with majesty.

Our second cause for discomfort (that's code for pain) arises from a nine day celebration of the Virgin of Guadalupe. Now, despite my religious affiliation as agnostic, I respect the spiritual displays of others. However, this particular "display" presents challenges. Each morning around 5 a.m. three or more M80s are detonated. Each evening around 6:30 p.m. the same artillery is deployed only in greater numbers. Every six legged, four legged or no legged creature responds with blood reddened eyes, a panic-stricken demeanor and burrows deep within the ground. Nikki simply disappears under the bed for the duration. She and I count the days together; passage of time is measured by the twice daily booming.

Virtually all cultures employ some form of fireworks to animate their festivals. Observances last a day or two or three. Perhaps during the upcoming Vatican Council, the cardinals might discuss the reality that virgins in today's world just don't last as long as they used to. Hence, the shortening of celebrations in their honor might warrant consideration.

A new Face Book page exists under the name of Yelapa Memo. It is dedicated to my writings on the blog and the Adventures with Teo series. A sample of the art work which enriches each edition is posted. Visit the page, "like" the page, click on the "get notifications" drop down and open your electronic door to great children's literature.

Will there be food to eat?

Yelapa is defined by its cycles. There are cycles with the tides, the moon, the crabs, the various game fish, the rains, and the heat. We even have a few motorcycles although they are really scooters.

Over the past three weeks the village enters the wind-down cycle. As temperatures and humidity cycle in, tourists cycle out. Persons uttering English occupy markets, restaurants and paths less frequently. One activity which enjoys an uptick is that of construction. Owners scamper to acquire materials and workers to employ before the monsoons arrive mid-June. Yelapa construction mantra: do not get caught with a supply of unused concrete once the rains arrive. Many an owner has fled at the last moment in search of a tarp to avert his 80 lb. bag of concrete from becoming an 80 lb. block of cement. The process is irreversible.

Never the less, tourism trickles throughout the summer. Reappearing mid-evening after the heat has broken, a few venture onto the pathways in search of dining options.

While most restaurants close for the

summer, there are opportunities. Four grocery stores in the central village, one up-river plus one behind the restaurants on the main beach remain open year round. I suggest you purchase provisions for breakfast and lunch from these establishments. If food storage is not available, then do what the majority of the world does------shop daily.

An excellent online resource is Yelapa Visitors Face Book page. Dinner out may require some advance planning.

Here are your options as of this writing:

Ray's Place	Tues-Sun 6-10pm
	Birria Sun 9-11am
Café Bahia	Fri-Wed 9am-1pm
Abuelos	Mon-Fri 6-10pm
Pollo Bollo	Thurs-Mon 6-10pm
El Manguito	daily
Hotel Lagunita	daily

Restaurants on the main beach, varied hours of operation

A number of small *taquerías* flourish in the evening. These pop up in every nook and cranny. Just follow your nose. Travelers; here's a heads up. These establishments are generally part of someone's home, a patio, a deck or spare room. They will not be lavishly appointed. Set aside cultural snobbery and enjoy real Mexican home-made food. Remember to ask what kind of *"agua fresca"* (fresh juice) they are offering. If you have never tried *agua de jamaica* (hibiscus), then you are in for a treat. It is the perfect non-alcoholic thirst-quenching beverage on a summer night.

A Star is Born!

Our balcony overlooks a barnyard. Its residents include; chickens, both large and small, aged and young; black, brown, white and multi-colored, roosters and hens; one mule, the occasional cow and/or calf; two groups of garrobos, three dogs, one green iguana and the odd quartet of vultures who swoop in each morning to investigate the newly deposited spread of compost. The area's tranquility is periodically punctuated by a traversing *moto*, a child disbursed to collect eggs or an adult who sweeps leaves from atop the hardened soil. It is generally a picture of placidity.

Of late, two new sounds are audible from my perch. One is the muffled sound of an infant crying. A new daughter arrived across the way. She is a welcomed addition to the village in general and to her parents in particular.

The second of these audible events is decidedly unique. A week ago, the evening calm retreated as some unknown individual plopped onto an adjustable stool and began to brutalize a cow bell and a snare drum. The rhythm which emerged, clank-bam-bam, clank-bam-bam, clank-bam-bam continued for a quarter of an hour without interruption. My Pollyanna-ish approach to life nudged me to the conclusion that whatever parent had purchased this percussion set would instantly realize their error and have the original box repacked and awaiting the 7:45 a.m. water taxi for return to Puerto Vallarta. I retired that evening having experienced yet another slice of Yelapa life.

The following morn, the sun arises, the birds sing, and tiny wavelets lap. The morning taxi departs yet I do not spot any large box upon its bow. At 1:30 p.m. sharp, just as I am about to pair the first *totopo* laden with fresh guacamole with a sip of *Pacifico*, all serenity slips away. The drum demon returns, only it brings a friend. Another misguided parent has purchased a beginning level electric guitar. The joining of these two musical revelers is ordained. In the interest of complete disclosure, I must add that the guitar player has already mastered two chords prior to arriving (varoom and varaam). Jam sessions arise organically throughout the day. They are typically no more than fifteen minutes in length—thank gawd! The combination of dulce tones is predictable: clank-bam-bam (varoom), clank-bam-bam (varaam). You get the picture. I see an increase in kayak trips in my near future.

Holy, Moly!!! (June)

It is Monday morning; I consume my weekly ration of *birria*! Wait a minute, I hear my readers screaming. *Birria* is a Sunday event, right? Well, usually yes. The first weekend in June, is perhaps the busiest, seventy-two hours in Yelapa.

The sequence of events tracks something like this: Thursday night the bulls for the rodeo arrive and run through town; Saturday morning, locals as well as visitors from surrounding pueblos amass to participate in *Día de la Marina* (Marina Day). It is one giant beach party with lots of sun, fun, sauce (beer) and salsa. Evening arrives and every woman between seven and seventy sprints home, dawns the tightest pair of jeans they can pour themselves into, pulls cowboy boots out of a closet, slaps on some sexy little sleeveless plaid top, and off they trek to the rodeo arena. They are going to watch the bulls, right? Sunday morning finds the entire beach scenario repeating sans rodeo.

My venture down the main path this

morning, finds our village nearly in its usual state. One Captain is out washing his boat, readying it for the next charter; Leticia's market is open with staff sweeping the aisles from the prior day's traffic, and alas, Ray's enormous grin welcomes me for *birria*. Not a bad place to be on a Monday morning.

In the interest of full disclosure, I must acknowledge that I pass three *vaquero* clad gents with their heads down as they collectively support the wall behind them. Whether or not they have been immobile since early morning is irrelevant. Two others, similarly clad, experience difficulty in ambulating from Point A (their present position) to Point B (anywhere other than their present position) without having the line of travel appear more like an arc. Alas, they are peaceful and bother no one.

Soon the bulls will retreat, the beach will be scoured free of litter, the *panga* used as the beer dispensing booth will be pushed back into the sea. Yelapans will bask in yet another party perfectly purveyed. This is not the time, however, to take an extended break. Historically, the rainy season announces itself with a vengeance on/or about June 15. At some pre-ordained celestial moment, the land crab migration begins within a fortnight of the first rains. Several scouts have already been spotted charting routes.

That brings me back to Ray's. My three *birria* tacos adorn a rectangular plate, a cup of consommé steams while a cold Bloody Maria sweats profusely onto the plastic table cloth beneath. Ray, in an outward display of respect to locals/visitors alike, and in an inward display of brilliance, re-scheduled his weekly culinary event so as not to compete with the other major activities. What a guy, he's my *compadre*!

Rains Arrive

My *birria* tacos apparently re-constituted. My otherwise svelte profile now imitates that of the Happy Buddha. Alas, life is good on a Sunday morning in Yelapa.

The rains arrive, albeit a week early. Our village experiences three consecutive nights of significant precipitation. One enterprising soul trenches from the lagoon to the bay so the two bodies of water now ebb and flow in unison. The rains flush the silt from the mountains into the Tuito River. The river flows through the lagoon and into the bay altering an otherwise emerald green hue into a light chocolate brown. I prefer the emerald green.

The crabs that remained dormant for two years await some celestial signal to depart their land caverns. Scouts already pay the ultimate price of exploration. Their diminutive carcasses adorn intermittent cobblestones along the path. Once the major migration commences, their numbers swell a thousand fold. I sense this activity is one of seeking a mate versus sprinting into the surf. These are land-based buggers. All animals deserve a moment of happiness, right?

This will be a week of preparation as Nikki and I gather belongings for our summer trek to the North. We leave behind great friends, great food and 80 percent humidity. San Diego will welcome us with great family, a nearly one year old grand-daughter, the warm and tender touch of my wife, and four of Nikki's canine cousins. We're all good on the first three; Nikki is lukewarm on the last.

Yelapa Green

Yelapa is green. The verdant jungle embraces the village like a parent swaddling a squirming child. As the rains establish their routine, trees, plants, vines and shoots discard former browns and beiges and transition into Yelapa green.

I sense that the more primitive a culture, the more environmentally aware and protective it is. Impose the concepts of modernization and progress and voilà along trek the dark twins of pollution and degradation. Yep, that is progress, right? Let us consider a solitary item and its impact on Yelapa: individual sized containers of purified water. Without performing actual bottle counts and only judging by the cases seen disembarking the re-supply *pangas*, my best guess is that there are several hundred individual bottles of water sold, consumed and discarded weekly. As evidence of our greenness, we place collection receptacles throughout the community.

A number of the discards are collected; others are tossed into streams to be washed into the bay, others are pitched on the path to be flattened by passing *motos* while others are simply flung among the plants which line the walkways. The collection containers are emptied weekly, the contents consolidated at the town pier for return to Puerto Vallarta. My comments here are not intended to diminish the intent of those involved in this project. My intent is to proffer the understanding that while displaying outward acts of greenness; we fail to address the underlying cause; the creation of large amounts of discardable trash.

Yelapa Green-Part 2

In a prior post, I broached the topic of Yelapa's degree of environmental greenness/friendliness; using counter-measures most likely established by those responsible for assailing the environment in the first place. These included: recycling, energy efficiency and the protection of native plants and animals. Not surprisingly, each of these three components birthed a plethora of profitable industries. We now enjoy collection centers throughout most towns; these are then serviced by massive garbage collection-type vehicles that transport recyclables to some distant processing center. A deluge of expensive, energy-efficient products pass into consumers' hands. We revel that a product is "more efficient" yet we lack any awareness about the overall energy "footprint" associated with the raw materials, production, or subsequent transportation. We simply delight in displaying our new twenty speed blender.

Yelapa's electricity is provided by CFE *(Comisión Federal de Electricidad)*. The village has enjoyed electrical power for almost fifteen years. Prior to that, businesses (i.e. markets, a hotel, restaurants, some lodges, and homes) met their needs via generators. Individual generators are noisy, pollute, require repairs and periodic service and need a convenient supply of fuel. Those without generators either used kerosene lanterns or simply embraced the cycles of the sun.

The Mexican government considers Yelapa an impoverished zone. As a result, electricity is provided to the village at a fifty percent discount. Rumors surface that this benefit may be removed since Yelapa's main industry is tourism, not fishing, and that just possibly villagers are not as impoverished as earlier believed. The providing of deeply discounted electrical power is an economic and logistical boon to the village. It also removes any incentive to monitor overall energy costs. Previously these include fuel, lubricant, parts, service, transportation and handling. Now all you have to do is await your bi-monthly statement.

Nonetheless, Yelapans are frugal. Construction is expensive due to material transportation costs. Sand/gravel, the single exception to this, is extracted nearby from the Tuito River bed. Unlike American domiciles, the number of electrical outlets and light fixtures are normally no more than one or two per room. The only running appliance, excluding the odd boom box or an oscillating fan, is a small refrigerator. As of this writing Yelapa sports one ductless air conditioning installation and less than a hand full of portable/window units.

There is no centralized delivery system for natural gas. Villagers purchase individual propane tanks. Due to transportation costs, propane is expensive. More lodging operators and homes are installing on-demand water heaters instead of the gas/electric units. In addition to reducing consumption, this design also eliminates the chance of an unnoticed, extinguished pilot since there is no ignition until a demand is placed on the system.

There are no cars or trucks and never will be. Yelapa is home to perhaps thirty *motos* (ATVs), a hand full of small displacement scooters and one electric golf cart. All but one of these vehicles are gasoline powered and produce toxic emissions. To some villagers, the growing popularity of *motos* is a concern. To their credit, many haul heavy goods (i.e. bottled water, ice, concrete, cinder block, rebar, scrap, luggage), while others transport heavy adults and their hefty children to/from school daily.

Pack animals still haul building materials. A few use a mule for personal transportation. Most Yelapans walk from point A to point B and back again as did their forefathers/mothers. The old ways flex to accommodate the new ones that ironically seem less flexible. As of yet, those who return home to Yelapa have not declared that they "are strangers in a strange place." That is a good thing.

CHAPTER THREE
THE FOURTH YEAR

Back to Work   (October)

The next seventy-two hours will see clothes scrubbed, Nikki bathed and boxes stored. Then one tub, two totes, one dog crate and twin backpacks will be stuffed into an SUV for transport to the airport. The prior three days addressed the purchasing of toiletries, Nikki's annual visit to the Veterinarian, planning, organizing and much discourse. We are a busy trio.

Yelapans prepare for the upcoming season. They likewise scrub, bathe, store, stuff, and plan. All this is performed amidst much chatter. They are a busy bunch.

C-E-L-E-B-R-A-T-I-O-N   (November)

Our return week to Yelapa is always exciting. Reconnecting with friends, food, and village lifestyle demands a commitment of gargantuan proportions. Here's the itinerary:

Sunday
Arrive Puerto Vallarta International Airport @ 2:35 p.m. Clear Immigration, baggage claim, Vet check (for Nikki), Customs, then meet our pick-up by 3:30 p.m. Cash at the ATM, off to Los Muertos Pier to await the

water taxi. Arrive Yelapa Town Pier, connect with Sipriano to transport our travel bits up the hill to *Casa Azul*. Dash to Ray's Place for dinner by 6:30 p.m. Within ten minutes the world's best margaritas appear at our table and dinner is ordered. The rest is gastronomic history.

Monday

Due to the absence of foodstuffs at home, Diana and I enjoy breakfast (*machaca, huevos rancheros*) at The Eclipse. Breakfast fills the balance of the morning as we continue to meet/greet friends. We stop at Leticia's Market for groceries and return to *Casa Azul* to observe the Mexican tradition of the siesta. Arise, shower and head to *Tacos y Mas* for opening night. Pahuelas, greets us warmly and margaritas appear. Our eyes focus on the Five Taco Combination Platter. Diana and I take no taco prisoners tonight.

Tuesday

Unpacking continues at a leisurely pace. Another trip for groceries and a stop by The Eclipse for a take-away order of Tortilla Soup. Diana nurses the beginning of a migraine. The balance of the day quietly evolves.

Wednesday

A trek to the Town Falls mid-morning affirms the wonder surrounding us. Diana punctuates the experience with her totally abandoned imitation of a water sprite. More settling in; dinner at *Abuelos Taquería.* This is NOT your average taco stop. Abuelos is a full service restaurant which takes the humble taco and imposes designer level presence. Margaritas ordered, we settle in to select shrimp, octopus, marlin, crab or a mixed taco or quesadilla; all purveyed on handcrafted blue corn tortillas.

Thursday

I head for Yelapa Kayak Rentals. Minor cleanup on the platform before yaks can be lowered and scoured. A chime announces Diana's incoming call. I am beckoned to lunch; I must obey. *Siesta* time, shower time and down the hill we trek to Ray's Place. Mixed *fajitas* for me and a chicken burger for Diana. Three hours evaporate before we open the door to *Casa Azul.* We are at peace.

Friday

Over morning coffee, Diana is immobilized with guilt and declares that we cannot continue defining our lives in Yelapa by mere sleeping, eating and drinking. The time has come to be productive. My analytical side discerns that we are five days into a six month stay and raises the concept of whether or not this is a battle worth fighting. My creative/emotional side, in contrast, wants to holler "WTF" and declare that I am perfectly content to sleep/eat/drink through the remaining stay afforded by our Tourist Visa (180 days). I turn lovingly to my bride of nearly twenty-five years and respond "yes dear."

Saturday
    John and Tamara, arrive from Alaska for their first in a series of intermittent monthly stays. They request our company for dinner. Where? Ray's Place, of course! Great drinks, great food, great company.

Sunday
    You know the drill, right? *Birria* at Ray's Place. It is the first *birria* to cross Diana's lips in nearly nine months, while my absence totals a mere five months. Our eyes connect and we quietly commence the mantra of "yum."

A Moment of Contrasts   (December)

   Grey clouds blanket Yelapa. Nikki and I observe our morning rituals. A barely audible tap-tap-tap joins us and signals the onset of gentle rain. We exchange glances. She returns to her sprawl across the tile floor. I to my cup of coffee.

   A trek to the window confirms the totality of a gray bay, surrounded by gray mountains topped by gray clouds. All in contrast to typically rich beige sands licked by emerald waters, framed by a dozen shades of jungle green.

The off-centered morning is doubly punctuated by the fact that my best friend, creative partner and wife, Diana, is absent having departed yesterday afternoon. The succeeding forty-eighty hours always invite shared looks of "What's missing in this picture?" between Nikki and me. Previous posts addressed this near annual phenomenon.

A shuffle in the giant avocado tree reveals a clutch of cacique birds. They are the most beautiful of birds to call Yelapa home. A foot in length, they sport jet-black bodies accented by banana yellow striping. A black crest tops their elegant presence. I watch.

It is a moment of contrasts, blandness to beauty. I, like any other writer, approach my laptop and create. (The following is lifted from a recent Face Book post.)

"Those of faith, and those of not, find this time of year an opportunity to take stock. Outwardly our world is fraught with fear and frenzy, yet these are political issues. Through the entryway of any living space on this planet you will find real people in search of meaning to their lives, safety for their families, and an improved future for all. It is a shared core. . . . . "

Welcome 2015   (January)

We inhabit a planet with war, disease and famine. Such has always been and will always be. We live lives imbued with events ranging from minute to magnificent. (Ditto on the always been/always be) What defines each beginning is the mix we place into our emotional/intellectual bowl for the balance of the year. No two years are alike since each is an evolution/accumulation of those previously logged. Right?

MEMO AWARDS 2014

These "awards" were launched three years ago as an opportunity to feature many of my favorite food/service providers. There is no statistical analysis performed, no voting body to contend with and certainly no gold embossed envelopes to recycle. There is only I! (Yes, that is the correct grammar) New categories are added each year. Let's proceed.

Best Services Category:
Water Taxi/Captain--Prieta Linda/Capt. Neto
Baggage Porter/Trash Hauler-Sipriano
Market with the Greatest Number of Family Members Working at any One Time--Leticia's

Kayak Rental Operation-Yelapa Kayak Rentals (*La Playita*-the little beach)

Best Places Category:
Places to Visit in Yelapa (in order)--Town Waterfall, The Main Beach, The Big Waterfall

Best Food Category:
Breakfast Burrito on the bay--Cafe Bahía
Machaca, Tortilla Soup--Eclipse
Pozole (Monday night only)--Ramona's
Mixed Seafood taco, burrito in a Blue Corn Tortilla--Abuelos
Birria (Sunday morning and holidays)-Ray's Place

Overall Fabulous Food and drink--Ray's Place

There they are folks, congratulations to all. If you would like additional information, visit TripAdvisor.com

Waxing Poetic   (February)

Rains visited last evening to linger through mid-day.

Birds remain undisturbed. Pelicans attack the water's surface seeking any hint of fish below. Vultures, in pairs, occupy palm branches and perform exhaustive preening, which drier conditions preclude. Only the Great Frigate

Birds are absent.

Rio Tuito redeploys sand from banks redefined. Current courses bank-to-bank ferrying fallen coconuts like countless bobbing heads; then melds with the bay in a final fit of turbulence. Coffee colored fluid flushes forward to re-image an otherwise emerald bay.

Cobblestones embedded in village pathways revert to earlier grandeur as river rock.

Clouds attack and withdraw on Frostian paws over ridge lines near and far.

A lone yacht resides beyond my window. Occupants stare landward as local eyes stare seaward in return.

Stress imposed by a morning commute; appointments requiring re-schedule, errands unable to complete; all of these issues are non-events. If you need to venture outside, simply expand the uniform: (T-shirt; board shorts, baseball cap) to include a large, customized garbage bag.

   It's a great day to be a Yelapan---indoors.

Pelicans a Plenty

Below my window, a pod of pelicans harvests fish from the bay. They glide an eye lash width above the ocean, rise and stall, then extend fully into plopping posture and descend. Countless iterations occur prior to the setting of the sun. Flight patterns crisscross without incident. Each is accompanied by one or two assistants, a blue-footed booby or perhaps a brown turn. Flanking either side of the great-ballooned cavity, they peck, pry and pluck any morsel available.

At the mouth of the Rio Tuito, a pair of father/son teams performs the ancient art of casting a weighted net. First the rhythmic delivery by the father as he twists his torso, then casts. The net descends onto the water in perfect circular form. It sinks, is retrieved and prepared for a subsequent toss. The second is likewise executed with grace and perfection. The young apprentice is beckoned. His slight stature invites a struggle through each step of the process. This only looks easy at the hands of a master. The lad gathers the net clumsily, twists his body and stumbles, awkwardly launches a tangle of nylon and lead, then bows his head in embarrassment as the mass drops unopened only a short distance away.

Further across the beach are another father/son team. Each manipulates a hand line. The device defines brilliant engineering at its simplistic best. The equipment requires a donut sized spool, a length of monofilament and a weighted hook or lure. The lure is rapidly swung overhead and then cast into the sea as the open spool faces forward. The retrieval process is accomplished through rhythmic intermittent tugs, a pause, then more tugs. Each fisherman develops a distinct pattern.

The pod of pelicans remains below my window. They buoy and bob in the afternoon swells.

Donors Be Aware

During my four-year stint in Yelapa, I have met, greeted, chatted and dined with countless visitors. At some point in conversation, the topic will fall to giving/donating to the community. While outwardly, Yelapa presents as a beautiful, time-forgotten, leisure locale along the coastline of Banderas Bay, there are areas of need. These "areas" include health, education and the environment.

Yelapa is home to a beautiful health clinic, which also serves neighboring communities. As a growing population requires expanded health services, the community owned clinic finds itself in need of greater quantities of medical consumables as well as diagnostic equipment. Long-term visitors and locals remain abundantly charitable. The benefits of such charity are identifiable and far-reaching throughout several communities. Their services are featured on the Face Book page *Centro de Salud-Yelapa.*

Yelapa offers a pre-kinder thru high school educational opportunity. Funding beyond basic brick and mortar is scarce. Essential student supplies are always in demand. Aline Shapiro, a trusted, long-term visitor, together with a cadre of volunteers, converted a spare classroom at the elementary school into a library/media center for the children. These ladies now bring the gift of literature and so much more to the next generation of Yelapans. The benefits are immediate and identifiable. Age appropriate mono-lingual (Spanish) or bi-lingual (English/Spanish) books are welcomed. Amazon gift certificates are easily converted into needed supplies. Their Face Book page is *Biblioteca Yelapa.*

Yelapa outwardly offers visitors the appearance of a pristine bay defined by the lush jungle rising above the high tide mark. Look just beyond this point and you determine that the "pristineness" is subject to daily assault and degradation. Gray water is directed into the path of the Tuito River from the time it begins its flow through the mountains south of us. Septic systems built decades ago to service a single dwelling, now accept effluence from the three or more units built above the original structure. Candy wrappers, chip bags, plastic juice containers line our paths having been discarded earlier by little hands of children consuming empty calories from nutritionally void snacks. Local families/markets strategically display such items along the path to/from school. No money required here, other than early education as to healthy diet, and environmental sustainability.

A word/s regarding donor caution; a well-intentioned visitor is likely to be exposed to other soft requests for donations. These range from assistance with medical bills to supporting some personal cause. Do your homework. Research whether your contribution will benefit one individual or many. In most cases, avoid giving cash. It cannot be tracked and has proven ripe for abuse in the past. In reference to assisting an individual with their medical bills, know the person either directly or through someone you trust. If you assist, contribute in a way that is comfortable to you.

"There is no knowledge which is not power." (Mortal Combat II)

CHAPTER FOUR
RETIRING IN YELAPA

Will I be safe?

Safety and security are priorities. Yelapa is home to perhaps one hundred fifty ex-pats or repeat long-term visitors who not only feel safe in Yelapa, but who acknowledge that they feel safer here than they do from wherever they departed. Puerto Vallarta is a city of nearly one quarter of a million people. The airport on any given day during the high season processes more than eight thousand passengers. Now, those are significant numbers. In contrast, Yelapa has no airport, and "processes" perhaps one hundred visitors per day. The bulk of these stay a few hours.

The Gato Institute (spoiler alert, I'm about to get creative) has identified that your chances of experiencing felonious activity in Yelapa are less probable than being snuffed by a descending coconut. Unsubstantiated accounts worldwide place the annual frequency of that event around 15,000 times versus a worldwide population of 7,000,000,000. You do the math!

Tell any family member that you are traveling to a remote village in Mexico and be prepared to defend your current, as well as historical sanity. What about the murders drugs, kidnapping, squalor etc. etc. etc.? Calmly ask if they are familiar with similar issues within their own zip code. Do a little homework and then share the salient data. End of conversation.

The appearance of safety and security should not be an excuse to relinquish your logic, intelligence or common sense. You would not scatter valuables in full view in any hotel room in the States, why would you do it here? Many lodging managers offer security boxes or safes for your valuables, most of which should remain at home in the first place. Keep in mind, your American Passport is one of the most coveted documents in the world. Treat it as a high value item.

Dining and entertaining here is a casual exercise. Leave the "glam" at home, those are the people you bought it for anyway, right? If you stroll the streets of Yelapa appearing to have exited Neiman Marcus followed by a quick dash through Tiffany's, you'll only look foolish. If you stroll the streets of any large city in the world sporting the regalia mentioned above, then you're marking yourself as a target. Gender has no bearing.

Physical safety is no less important than your personal security. I alert visitors that

Yelapa is not a destination for anyone with mobility issues. Paths are constructed of rounded river rock. A sprinkling of sand or moisture renders the dry surface slick. An extended walk will require that you summit one or more hills. Rental properties owe spectacular views to the fact that you ascend fifty plus steps prior to unlatching your front door.

Keep your wits about you whenever you travel. If you feel uncomfortable in a situation back home, you retire to safety, ditto for when you travel. You venture to Yelapa to enhance your list of great experiences. Avoid some personal lapse of sensibility which allows friends to utter a giant "I told you so."

Do I need to speak Spanish?

Any high school freshman who survives the first week of foreign language class, understands the meaning of terror. Daily vocabulary lists, regular verbs to conjugate, irregular verbs to conjugate and the Friday conversations to compose and present. My high school's offerings included Spanish, French, German and the ever popular, Latin. I sense that the early slogging in one foreign language classroom is no different than in any of the others. Unlike college, you could not run to the counselor after the first class session and beg to be dropped. You were in for the year, end of discussion.

In retrospect, if you garner a "C" or better the first year, you feel linguistically invincible. And in a moment of temporary insanity, and at your parent's prodding, you agree to return the following year. The instruction makes sense. The affective filter drops and the weekly conversations become fun. Years three and four explore the cultures of those countries who speak the language. Fridays become a virtual play day as most of the period is spent singing Mexican folk songs. By the end of a two year stint in community college, I rack up another four Spanish classes with no intention of ever employing my skills.

Post script: I subsequently utilize my Spanish skills on virtually every job, in every location in the world, and now find myself living in a Mexico whose language and culture I studied nearly fifty years ago.

Yelapa is a village of twelve hundred year-round Mexican residents. North Americans have visited since the 1960s. Those locals who are able financially, send their sons and daughters for multiple year stays with relatives in California, primarily the San Jose and Santa Cruz area. The purpose of the journey is to learn English. Virtually anyone involved with the visiting public, speaks some English. You buy groceries, rent kayaks, order dinner and ask directions to the waterfall with nothing more than the language skills you already possess.

Now, having said that; why not learn a few key words in Spanish, just to let your hosts know you value their culture? As a former bilingual educator, here is the approach I suggest. Purchase a basic English-Spanish dictionary. Make a list, in English, of twenty nouns (things) that you need to know (i.e. beer, bathroom, beach, table, keys, shirt, pants, etc.). Fold a new piece of paper in half lengthwise; cut out a picture of the word and place it on the left half; across from the picture write the word in Spanish. English does not appear. Your brain will associate the picture with the Spanish word. Add to this list the basics of *hola* (hello), *adios* (good bye), *gracias* (thank you). *buenos dias/tardes/noches* (good morning/afternoon/night) and you are good to go. If you need to create a question using one of your listed nouns, simply voice an inflection following the word. For example; you want to ask Where is the beach? Simple, the noun is playa, your question becomes "playa?" *Buenas suerte!* (good luck)

A Healthy Life

Yelapa offers a healthy life style. You have to elect to participate. I walk wherever I go. Twice a day, I take Nikki, our English Shepherd, into the jungle for a break. Two or three times a week I walk to the grocery store. Three or so nights a week I walk to dinner. Nearly every day, I walk to my kayak stand, sweep the platform, spiff the kayaks, and enjoy the view. While many of the twenty/thirty something males have *motos* (ATVs), the rest of us walk and walk and walk. I lose ten pounds in the first six months. My physical stamina is better than when I was twenty-five years younger. Did I mention that Yelapa has hills? Yes, it is a physical environment.

Food and beverages taste better. Drinks/smoothies are crafted one at a time with fresh ingredients. Fruits, vegetables, poultry, fish, beef, pork and baked goods are fresh. There is a distinct absence of processed foods in markets or on menus.

Medical Care

The availability of quality medical care is something most people feel should be a right. So you're thinking, why would anyone in their proper mind move to a remote Mexican village, forty-five minutes away from a major medical facility? I thought you'd never ask.

Yelapa is home to a spacious medical clinic managed by *Seguro Popular*, a Mexican health insurance provider. Think of it as an urgent care facility. The clinic is staffed by two medical doctors and a certified nurse. All minor medical issues can be addressed. Major medical issues are referred to Puerto Vallarta. Pre-natal care is offered. Deliveries are not performed. All in need are welcome, locals and visitors alike. No visitor is turned away or asked to pay for any service provided. Having received medical attention at the clinic on two occasions, I know the staff to be professional, courteous and helpful. I always leave a donation with the receptionist. Should major emergency care be required after 6 p.m., the person is transported to Puerto Vallarta on a designated emergency water taxi.

Puerto Vallarta offers medical opportunities afforded much larger cities. Since fees are substantially less, PV has become a destination for medical tourism. This attraction stretches well beyond elective surgeries. It includes dental work or consultations from every specialty imaginable. It is not uncommon for doctors in the Western United States to maintain offices in Puerto Vallarta. Their primary focus is serving the medical needs of the North American traveler. The reception areas, consultation areas and the professional service provided match or exceed hospitals stateside.

Puerto Vallarta hospital websites appear below. I urge you to spend time with each. If you have ongoing medical issues or are contemplating an upcoming medical event, each hospital invites your inquiry as to the extent of service provided and the associated costs. They are in alphabetical order:

Hospital Amerimed (www.amerimed.com.mx)
Hospital CMQ (www.hospitalcmq.com.mx)
HospitalMedasist (http://www.hospitalmedasist.com)
HospitalSanXavier (http://www.sanjavier.com.mx)

Dental health is part of wellness. Puerto Vallarta is home to a number of dental practices which cater to the North American traveler. We enjoy the service provided at Just Smiles (http://justsmiles.com.mx). It meets or surpasses anything which we experience in the States.

Here is a resource to consider whether relocating or just vacationing. Pamela Thompson, a former nurse of many years in California's Central Valley, runs an operation akin to a health services discount card. For a modest premium, she provides a raft of services (file keeping, appointments, lab work follow-up, insurance form translation and submission, plus she hosts an annual health fair attended by a huge portion of the Banderas Bay ex-pat community—at no cost to the attendee). Many of Puerto Vallarta's medical practitioners are present in the exhibit hall. In addition, the doctors within her "network" offer lesser fees to members. She receives no compensation from them. All of her income is derived from the sale of memberships. We are members and have used her referral system extensively. It is invaluable to enjoy that level of contact. Her primary website appears below:

HealthCareResources
http://healthcareresourcespv.com/home.html

A word about your existing medical insurance. Before departing, determine if your coverage extends to international travel. Is there a limit to the number of days you can be away from your home country? Ask about the procedure for filing a claim should you require medical services abroad. Medicare will not reimburse you for medical expenses incurred outside of the USA. The Veteran's Administration does have a product for international travelers but you cannot be out of the USA for more than thirty consecutive days. Find out before you travel. Pamela Thompson can answer your questions about Mexican medical insurance.

If I have identified that a medical entity "caters" to the North American traveler that simply means that everyone involved is fluent in English. Now, take a breath.

Can I Visit My Money?

All my banking needs can be handled via one plastic card at an ATM (*cajera automatica*). Our home bank is located in Southwest New Mexico. My wife, Diana, spends a portion of the year in Southern California, and I reside in Mexico. Neither of us has seen the inside of our branch in years.

Unless you operate a business in Mexico, THERE IS NO REASON TO OPEN A MEXICAN BANK ACCOUNT. Mexican banking regulations, restrictions, etc. are different from the States.

In advance of your stateside departure, alert your bank to your travels into Mexico (give them the date in and date out) and identify the need to use both debit and credit cards. Confirm your daily limits for cash withdrawals and/or purchases. Also, inquire as to your bank's fees relative to international transactions. Be forewarned that you may be charged on both sides; initially when the transaction is performed at the ATM in

Mexico and subsequently when the same transaction is processed by your home bank. If you determine that the fee situation is not to your liking, locate another institution that you can use as an intermediary for transferring funds electronically and subsequent withdrawal via debit card. Puerto Vallarta enjoys a presence of all major Mexican banks as well as many internationals. Cash advance fees range from $3.50 USD (BanNorte) to $5.00 USD (Bancomer). Some stateside banks then apply a $7.00 to $12.00 assessment once they process the same transaction. At that point, you just paid $15.00 USD in fees to complete your $200.00 cash advance.

I enjoy a relationship with a small credit union. I know the senior operations officer by first name. We communicate via email or phone when my wife or I migrate between California and Mexico. All my income is deposited electronically, (no charge), I am extended a VISA account at less than half the big bank rate (no annual fee), and international transactions are free (no fee). I pay my obligations online (no charge). What is there not to like about this relationship?

Mexican ATMs will generally display screens either in English or dual language format. Be sure to read each screen carefully. (Just a reminder that the amounts on the screen are Mexican pesos not American dollars) All of my transactions are performed in an air conditioned booth at *BanNorte* in the *Zona Romantica*. The bank is a five minute walk from Los Muertos Pier and on my route to the city buses. In addition to the comfort of an enclosed air-conditioned cubicle, the door locks behind me. This important feature affords privacy.

Remember there are no ATMs in Yelapa. Very few establishments (lodging, eating) accept credit cards. Plan to pay cash for everything. Insure that the cash remains on your person at all times. Travel wisely and you will be fine.

Enjoying a trip/stay in Mexico need not be daunting. Plan ahead with a cash reserve for the first week and enter the international direct phone numbers for contact people at your bank. What is that adage about a penny of prevention is worth a peso of cure? You'll work it out.

What size budget do I need?

This question obsesses silver panthers seeking the greatest bang for their retirement buck (*peso*). Numerous periodicals post annual "Top Ten Lists." An entire genre of printed material exists in the Senior Self-Help section of book stores. Perhaps lowest cost of living is your priority, however, there are a host of other issues you should consider.

Yelapa is an isolated village on the southern side of Banderas Bay. It can be reached from Puerto Vallarta via a forty-five minute water taxi trip or from Boca de Tomatlan by a twenty-five minute water taxi trip. There is a seasonal road into Yelapa used to transport building materials; EVERYTHING else arrives by boat.

Transportation contributes to the cost of groceries, building materials, lodging, dining and general living in our village. Stateside magazines score sites on low property taxes, the availability of a local university, a fully functional library, a major health facility, and the ever popular civic opportunities and volunteer organizations. Yelapa has none of these!

Another post "Rent or Build" discusses the general practice of annual prepaid rents. Depending upon individual taste, you can spend from $300 to $1000 per month on rent. Based upon your personal culinary needs you could spend $100 to $500 per month on groceries (wine/liquor excluded). The average dinner out to include one drink and tip averages $15 per person. There is no charge for providing water to your residence although you will wish to purchase bottled water for drinking at $2.00/bottle. Electricity is subsidized 50% by the electric company, CFE, and will run $40 to $80 every two months. Most ex-pats head over to Puerto Vallarta once a week or so ($20 round trip) to bank and shop (Costco, Home Depot, Walmart, Sam's Club, Office Depot, Staples, TelMex) or to attend to medical ($40/consultation)/dental appointments ($35/cleaning) There's your total. Add twenty-five percent and you will approach your monthly living cost in Yelapa.

Reality check: From the end of November through the end of April, Yelapa is one of the most spectacular places in the world. The heat/humidity/monsoonal rains roll in from May through October causing most ex-pats to flee to such spots as Calgary, Portland, San Diego or The Rockies. Having a second residence adds to your costs. Tip: consider approaching your adult children with the announcement that you look forward to re-connecting with them (and the grandchildren) for a six month extended stay each year. It's payback time folks.

Rent or Build

Only certain individuals may own property in Yelapa. A visitor may build and/or rent for a multi-year period (5 years). No classified ads exist. It is all by word of mouth. If you are interested, alert your lodging host prior to arrival and ask for guidance. In advance, identify your annual budget and cash available to make repairs/upgrades. A move or building project will always cost more than you anticipate; that's a fact! Allow a twenty-five per cent over-ride. Rent/lease payments are generally paid annually in advance. Keep in mind that you will be paying an annual rental amount on a location that you only wish to use six months of the year.

Building in Yelapa is expensive. Everything (brick, concrete, rebar, windows, tile, paint, appliances, furniture, fixtures, etc.) must be brought in by boat (*panga*). Each time someone handles/touches your materials, there are costs. These costs are difficult to estimate. Accept the mantra that "this is not the (the name of your country) and the related mantra "Do not spend more on a project than you can walk away from." Two must reads for those considering building in a foreign country are Jack Smith's *God and Mr. Gomez* and John Mole's *It's All Greek to Me!: A Tale of a Mad Dog and an Englishman, Ruins and Retsina.*

Costs, completion time, manner of payment, renter/landlord responsibilities, ability to sub-lease and follow-up work, among others, should be detailed in writing (both in English and Spanish) in advance. Be sure to address the issue of funding during the build out. Do you wish to be personally involved during the process, or will you fund from afar based upon evidence of performance? How will payment be made? Lastly, establish the builder's fee for performing and supervising the work. Nobody works for free.

If you are committed to creating a place of your own, consider an extended stay first. This grants you the opportunity to experience first-hand: weather, traffic, noise, access, proximity to shopping and departing transportation. Relocation is a huge task; it is not an extended vacation. Distinguish between the two.

If you elect to rent an existing space, then the event becomes slightly less complicated. Chances are you will wish to perform some improvements. Once that occurs, virtually all the items mentioned above apply. Likewise, consider an extended stay in your selected site. Then spend time in other areas around town. There are distinct differences among the four colonies. Barking dogs, crowing roosters or screaming children can tarnish any dream house. Renter be aware!

Contracts to rent/build range from oral to attorney prepared. Typically, by working with your landlord (through an interpreter if necessary) you can identify the issues. Keep it simple, Yelapans are not litigious sorts. At the end of the day, you want a place you can enjoy and share with others. Settling in and sorting out may take you the better part of the first year.

Transportation Fees

This concept is challenging for *gringos* to grasp. Stateside, we engage a contractor to complete an improvement. We sign a contract for a specific cost. Materials are purchased, delivered and consumed all within established parameters. Allow me, via example, to illustrate the Yelapan counterpart. Building materials are purchased from an outlet in Boca de Tomatlan, a twenty-five minute *panga* ride. Materials are carried out the door to a spot on the beach (fee); a *panga* is sent from Yelapa (fee); the materials are loaded (fee); the materials arrive in Yelapa and unload onto the beach (fee); pack mules or someone with a *moto* and a trailer loads the materials (fee); the driver brings them to the job site (fee); a crew unloads them (fee). All of these "fees" are paid in cash, no receipts. Depending on the material requirements of your job, this process repeats a dozen times. No one is being ripped off; it is just a different system. Transportation fees arise whenever your materials are "transported" from point A to point B; you get the idea, right?

Yelapa is a special place. It is not for everyone. Life here is physically demanding. Summer heat and humidity are oppressive. Most long-term visitors flee to cooler climes, although there are some who remain. Do your homework and always carry a flashlight at night.

EPILOGUE

Yelapa treats us well. Despite insects, arachnids and reptiles, we embrace the raw energy of nature as it exists a few steps out our front door. Four annual cycles have passed since our arrival. Amazing, warming, humbling, rewarding and enriching, all swirl in a tumbler of terms. Unquestionably, the majority of our experiences are positive, for that we say "thank you."

Once again, our nomadic spirits grow restless. It is time for the next adventure. We will archive the memories of all that is, and those who are Yelapa. In Spanish, there exist an open-ended nature to saying goodbye. It is built around the inference that all will meet again. *Que le vaya bien, Yelapa. Que le vaya bien.* (May all go well, Yelapa. May all go well.)

ABOUT THE AUTHOR

DW Risdon is a former banker turned English teacher. Along with his wife, Dianne, and their English Shepherd, Nikki, the trio relocated to Mexico. His blog, yelapamemo.blogspot.com features anecdotes of daily life in their adopted village of Yelapa.

His writings include the nine-edition bilingual children's series, *The Adventures with Teo-Las Aventuras con Teo.* Each is richly illustrated by Dianne Risdon.

- The Lonely Egret-*La Garceta Solitaria*
- Dogs of Yelapa-*Los Perros de Yelapa*
- The Farmers Market-*El Mercado*
- The Waterfall-*La Cascada*
- The *Pangas-Las Pangas*
- The Church-*La Iglesia*
- Fun in Yelapa-*Diversión en Yelapa*
- Trip to Puerto Vallarta-*El Viaje a Puerto Vallarta*
- The Popsicle Man-*El Paletero*

Beyond the Guano: A Yelapa Memoir

www.ingramcontent.com/pod-product-compliance
Lightning Source LLC
Chambersburg PA
CBHW071455040426
42444CB00008B/1351